# Art Heals

## *Stories About Healing and Collage*

by

## Liz McEntee

Painted Cottage Publishing

Painted Cottage Publishing Edition 2023
Copyright © 2023 Liz McEntee
Collage artwork copyright @ Liz McEntee
All rights reserved.
ISBN 979-8-9878897-0-1
Cover art by Liz McEntee
Cover design by GetCovers
Author photograph by Angela McEntee

*To the gifted, who would not sit down and did not shut up.*

story
My Dear Cousin Mary
Write Often as your packages
are more precious than Gold Dust
Nation
USA
29
SCORPIVS SAGITTA CAPRIC: AQVARI

Story.

# A Foreword

Liz McEntee has written a timely, practical, and moving account of the healing powers of art.

*Art Heals* is written in an engaging and vivid style, and it brims with solid and practical advice about healing the soul, mind, and emotions. Liz's book resonates with the authority of those who have gone through a great struggle with depression and emerged on the other side.

While acknowledging how healing is aided by others, Liz also encourages the empowerment of people to awaken their own inner power of healing. Specifically, Liz advocates collage-making as a healing tool.

Brimming with practical advice on how to use collage for healing, Liz encourages her readers to cast aside the doubts that inhibit our artistic impulses and tap into their inner creativity. Collage offers a way to express all the passionate intensity within us that is pushed down in the affliction we call depression. Liz details how collage work can be a creative and healing response to depression.

I loved her book and I encourage others to read it.

Reverend Ed Brock

Author

Interim Minister

Unitarian Universalist Fellowship

# Preface

I am a lifelong artist. Well, as soon as I figured out my fingers and toes. There was a break (I share it in this book), but except for that, I have always been an artist.

I am also a storyteller. As a storyteller, I love finding images and words that delight the audience and encourage them to consider new ideas.

I love color. I love cutting paper and gluing it into endless configurations. I love painting and pushing luscious hues across a canvas.

My earliest memory of drawing and coloring was making an elf family.

The youngest elf.

In 6th grade, I decided to enter the school art contest. I was carefully drawing a city street. Red apartment buildings filled the page along with trash-filled waste bins and playing kids. My friend asked me for help: What should she draw? We were using oil pastels, a medium that lends itself to easy blending and smudging. I suggested she use this to her advantage and create an abstract drawing. Giving her this suggestion left me with that warm sensation that comes from helping a friend. She got busy filling her page with colorful swirls.

My talent was publicly acknowledged when I ended up winning second prize. A photograph of my drawing was published in the local paper. First prize went to my friend for her color-filled abstract. I was very proud of my part in her victory. It convinced me that I had a knack for helping friends. And it reinforced my belief that I had a natural ability to make art.

My favorite place in grade school, junior high, and high school was the art room. The colors, the supplies, and the aromas all promised endless possibilities. Art rooms were a place of refuge, solace, and hope throughout my schooling.

Life could be unpredictable and threatening. But from an early age I found the atmosphere of the school's art studios to be soothing. The art rooms in the many schools I attended were sanctuary spaces for me before I even knew the word "sanctuary."

When a riot broke out at my junior high, I ran to the art room. The teacher had the presence of mind to lock us in. We could hear the mob of kids as they ran through the halls screaming and banging on the doors. In the art room we were safe.

Yes, art heals.

I began collaging in high school. Soon, making collages became my dependable companion, a form of Medicine and a way to share my voice. When I use a capital M on Medicine, I am referring to all things that lead us back to ourselves, that help us heal, that help us rejoin our spirit.

I am sharing my stories in hopes that they resonate with you. I encourage you to try new things and to play with color, paper, cutting, and gluing.

Let this time of experiment and play be Medicine. Let this Medicine give you back your voice. Let this Medicine lift your spirit. Let your voice whisper to you, let it bring you back to trusting yourself.

Why am I sharing my experiences? Because making collages saved me. While I am not a trained therapist, I have logged many hours with many therapists. Along with collage and therapy, I have used medication, exercise, diet (no sugar, no flour, vegetarian, all junk food), prayer, and meditation. I have journaled, shopped, slept, cried, and yelled. Each of these would distract me for a while from the grief and anger that lived in me – the grief that I felt would drown me and the anger that I felt would burn me up. "Where did all this grief and anger come from?" I asked myself.

It seemed to come from everywhere and nowhere.

Over the course of my journey, I have learned that healing from the darkest times requires persistence. Often your focus narrows to getting through the next 15 minutes or the next hour.

As I moved from crisis control to maintenance of the chronic conditions of depression and bipolar II, I needed to develop different skills. I still miss staying up too late painting and making art, crawling into bed covered in paint and bits of paper. However, I have seen the wisdom of learning how to have an orderly life. I have seen for myself that using all our tools (including a regular sleep schedule) creates a life that can be the masterpiece we deserve. After all, would we use only one shape, one color, one pencil, one tube of paint in our lives as artists? While these practices are not art supplies, they can allow you to prepare your inner fortitude to create.

1. Seek care from skilled people who can assist your recovery.
2. Go to your appointments.
3. Take your meds. (When you find the right meds, respect what they can do.)
4. Keep trying things. You will find what works.
5. Forgive yourself for being unlike others. There is no shame in being quirky. There is no shame in getting help. There is no shame in changing your helpers until you find the ones who treat you with respect and professionalism.
6. Respect your life force.

You may forget appointments. You may decide you don't want to take your medicine. You may not feel worthy – and that is why the first step is particularly important. Skilled people will know when to be patient and when to be firm. They will guide you as you heal. They can hold the knowledge that you are worthy until you grasp that truth.

My stories are offered as the extra sauce on your care plan. Your healing and care will involve a team. The people who make up your team will be guided by your best interests. It helps to have a variety of people with different skills and different approaches. Your team will change and evolve, which is to be expected. And even with the most caring team, even with days filled with therapy, exercise, meditation, and prayer, we are left with hours every day when we are on our own. Hours that we are left to ourselves to figure out what to do.

After all, therapists vacation, retire, and move. Friends, family, people of faith, neighbors... they also live their own lives, leaving you with time on your hands. That's what the Collage Calls to Action you find sprinkled through this book are all about. The Calls to Action are for times that you want something to occupy your mind and hands. For the times you need to do something that is low-risk but meaningful and rewarding. The times you want to follow your curiosity and explore your creativity.

I have struggled with depression for decades. During two urgent episodes I considered leaving this life. I've had passive thoughts such as "people who drive into telephone poles don't have any more problems."

Yet I am still here, living a life that is not what I expected and certainly not perfect. And I am extremely glad I stayed.

Over time, I embraced a personal philosophy that removed the option of suicide. I encourage everyone to value life and the experiences it brings. I encourage everyone to create a team to support you, valuing yourself and your life. My team is composed of doctors, therapists, energy workers, friends, family, teachers, guides, guardian angels, and a lineage of ancestors. These are living people and deceased people, known and unknown.

I encourage you to assemble your team of people – and a collage toolkit. Ask for help and stay the course.

Staying the course requires us to choose life. Repeatedly. In healing, you turn away from despair and toward living over and over again. Healing allows you to choose life as often as you need. I encourage you to stay here so we can continue to enjoy you and your gifts for as long as possible.

And for those who have lost loved ones, I offer my deepest condolences.

# Rock, Paper, Scissors. Oh, wait.
# Glue, Paper, Scissors!

Remember that game? We will play a variation with a win-win for all players.

To begin, what shall we put in our toolbox?

If you have supplies already, feel free to use what you have. Dig around in your closets, cupboards, and drawers. I have found delectable supplies that I had tucked away and forgotten. If you are interested in buying supplies, I have listed some that I have used and found to be reliable. Is there anything more aggravating than being inspired when your glue stick is dried out? Your scissors aren't sharp? Your pen won't write when you have a flash of inspiration? (Pro tip: If the pen isn't working, don't put it back with the other pens. Toss it.)

- **Uhu Stic glue sticks:** I've used many brands. Uhu lasts a long time, glides on nicely, and is easy to find.
- **Coccoina glue sticks:** This glue glides on like butter. It has a faint almond aroma, it is pricey, and it is not carried by as many vendors... but a web search will bring up retailers.

- **Cutter Bee scissors:** These are extremely sharp small scissors; they are excellent for fussy cutting when you're creating intricate shapes. Because these scissors are extremely sharp, they give a nice crisp cut. Designate one pair of scissors for cutting paper. They will cut paper well for a long time. But they won't give you a clean cut with fabric. Scissors can be sharpened professionally or at home.
- **Paper:** I will write more about paper in a bit. For now, I will admit to having a lot of paper in my house. A lot.
- **White gel pen:** Uni-ball Signo white gel pens write smoothly with a clear, strong line. As long as the surface you are writing on is dry, the Uni-ball Signo will write on most papers and painted surfaces. I recommend you cap your pen when it is not in use and store it horizontally for a longer life span.
- **Set of markers:** I like to use Crayola Pipsqueak Markers. They are water soluble. The basic set gives you nice colors, and you can often find it on sale..

The gifts that collage-making can bring to your life are not dependent on fancy supplies or materials. The gifts arise out of the act of making collages. And collages can be made from the most humble and unexpected materials.

Act Well: A collage made with security envelope paper, a fortune from a
fortune cookie, and a small sun image.

Eventually, as you pursue your love of collage, your list of supplies will include everything that strikes your fancy... paint, stickers, tape, string, ribbon, sticks, seeds, macaroni, envelopes, stamps, tickets, watercolors, brushes, journal pages, lists, books, oil pastels, pencils, photos, leaves, flowers, glassine envelopes, vellum, baggies, receipts, handwritten recipes, and random things that blow across your path when you are taking a walk.

But to start, let's use scissors, papers, and glue. Simple. Easy.

# Chapter 1

---

## *French Magazines as Medicine*

The late summer of 1983 found me in New Rochelle, NY, sitting on a green chenille thrift-store couch with scratchy cushions and elaborate tassels. My sister had bought it for $25. I was 26 years old, a grownup, supporting myself – but my life looked nothing like I thought it should. I'd come from Philadelphia to see my family for a two-week visit three years earlier. I hadn't decided to move back to NY. I was just putting off making decisions.

At 18, I had gotten into my first-choice college – an art school in Philadelphia. But by my sophomore year I had gradually stopped going to class. I stopped doing art. I gave away my supplies. I told everyone I was not an artist.

As I write this chapter, I am considering how to explain my choices.

I had left for college with more bluff than life skill. My make-believe self-confidence was delicate, prone to rips and tears. As the months went by, I realized I had no idea how to shop for food, no idea how to cook meals, no idea how to spend 24 hours a day with the 10 other artists who lived on my floor in the dorm.

I was not prepared to go from being an admired senior in the high school art department to one of many anonymous freshmen at a private art college. I was unprepared for each new experience, and each one destroyed a bit more of my facade. I felt like the cardboard scenery in an off-off-Broadway musical. No one expected the play to last long enough to require anything sturdier. A window falls to the ground. A streetlight stops working. The door sticks until someone finally just rips it down.

As my dream of a happy college experience was ground down by reality, someone seemed to have hired a songwriter to compose a musical score: music in a minor, discordant key with the tempo of a slow dirge. The unrelenting lyrics reinforced my fears that I was unworthy, broken, unlovable, and unwanted.

I had no healthy self-soothing skills. It would be years before I even heard about healthy self-soothing skills. I was unable to communicate what I wanted or needed. In fact, I didn't know what I needed. Barking seals in a circus sideshow were more articulate than I was at the time. I moved through life terrified that people would realize how messed up I was. And I believed that I would be sent to one of the bleak insane asylums that were still operating at the time.

Juggling all of this had brought me to the point of exhaustion. I was no longer able to pretend to be normal like everyone else. I was crying all the time, bracing against black moods and torturous thoughts. I knew this was how it would always be. It would never get better. I would never feel better. Life would never be better. I sat on that scratchy thrift-store couch and told my sister that I was done, that I couldn't take it anymore, that there was no point in living.

If you are lucky and have never felt depressed, imagine that you are wearing a 50-pound backpack walking through thigh-high sand for days and weeks on end. You are accompanied by a companion who says, "You are worthless, people would be better off if you were gone, no one loves you" on an endless loop while you have a low-grade flu and you ache all over and you are processing decisions with the skill of a 5-year-old.

My sister said a lot of things that day but the thing that saved my life was when she said, "Look, you don't have to do anything. You don't have to accomplish anything at all ever again. But please don't hurt yourself."

It's hard to describe what a gift that was, how freeing her words were. If you don't have to do anything but eat, breathe, and sleep, life is so much easier.

Over time I grew to see how my low moods were built upon stories I told myself. One of the big stories was that I was failing at life. Dismantling this cruel and inaccurate story was a long-term project. In fact, while drafting this book, I found myself still peeling back more layers.

The pivotal message was about expectations, being genuine, accepting where I was and being accepted where I was.

There are people who have millions of dollars but do not have anyone to tell them, "It's ok that you aren't able to keep up your pretenses. We just care about you." And there are poor people who are accepted for who they genuinely are. So don't get hung up on specific details of your "failure" or "success."

As I share my story and what I've learned over the last sixty-plus years of studying my depression, my despair, my soul, and my healing process, consider who accepts you and where you are. Focus on who makes you feel calmer or more accepted. Notice who makes you feel worse. Spend more time with the people who add value to your life. Spend as little time as possible with the people who find their joy in upsetting you. In fact, get them out of your life as soon as possible.

Having money is awesome. Having true friends is one of the best gifts you can give yourself. And having both opens up connection and freedom, a fabulous combination. Embrace it. Revel in it.

The conversation with my sister delivered immediate relief. It's not that I jumped up from the couch, ran a marathon, built a successful career, got married, and became the best version of who I thought I should be. No, I am still a work in progress. What I mean is that I shut the door on the option of killing myself.

In fact, untangling the confusion of who I was took a long time. Shortly after this conversation, I had a reading with an astrologer, Maria Napoli. She told me the next two years would be tough but then I would feel much better. The next two years were tough. I spent many nights lying in bed planning my visit to her at the two-years-and-one-day mark. I would stomp into her apartment and yell at her. "You fucking lied to me!" But she was right.

The good news about bad years is that you live them one minute at a time. And even in the worst year of your life, there are moments of grace and love and art.

After my sister gave me permission to be a total failure, she handed me my birthday present: three French fashion magazines that she had brought back from her trip.

It was the best birthday present I could have been given at that time. She remembered that I loved making collages. These magazines were perfect. They were French, meaning fancy, foreign, fascinating, and inexplicable - I wouldn't get bogged down in reading them. There were three of them, enough to have material to play with for a long time – but not so much that it would overwhelm me. And most importantly, the magazines gave me an effortless way to get back to making art.

I was able to scrounge up glue and white paper (I used the white paper as substrate – substrate being the fancy word for the paper that holds the collage) and I began making collages again. I could make art without having to call myself an artist. Without the pressure to be someone successful and important, I could enjoy the act of cutting or tearing out photos and gluing them down on paper.

I had been enticed out of the pit of despair. The activity was not threatening, but familiar. Making collages helped me clear away negative thoughts, leaving space in my head for clarity.

I started thinking about other ways to heal. At first, I simply enjoyed the physical act of cutting, tearing, and gluing. But soon it was clear that collages were offering hints, suggestions, questions, and answers. My body and soul knew these things even when my mind was confused.

As the months went by, I crept back into the world. I got a job escorting high school kids to an after-school program for the local grade school. I despised the high school students; their gossip and world weariness were a bit too familiar. But I loved to hang out with the grade school kids. I enjoyed their energy, their curiosity, and their artwork. They were still open to life and to awe. My enthusiasm was obvious. The high schoolers put in the prescribed hour and left. I stayed until the young children went home. At the end of the school year, the program director offered me a job in the fall.

Spending afternoons with the little kids was effortless. Compare that to spending 30 minutes making sure the high schoolers all got on the bus that carried them to their volunteering sites. Every high schooler was ticking a box on a long list of "how to get into the best college" activities. The time I spent with them did not lift my energy. Ever.

But the younger kids, especially the 5-year-olds, engaged my curiosity and creativity. That lifted my energy, and the lift lasted well beyond the afternoon. Like a blind dog sniffing for a treat, I pursued a hit-or-miss path toward self-healing. The path often led me into more collisions than moments of healing. But it was the best strategy I had for propelling myself forward. I tried to notice where the scent got stronger and I hoped for the best as I bumbled along toward it.

During the dark times, your healing path will not be obvious. If it were obvious, we would all be on our paths. We might feel sad, but we wouldn't feel lost or hopeless.

Imagine you are starting a journey. As you walk along, most people misdirect you.

Some steer you wrong because they are idiots. They may be well-meaning idiots, but you are now off course. Others misdirect you because they are selfish. Some want to see you suffer. Others are afraid of anyone who seems different, and they hope to lose you if they can point you down a cold dark lonely path. There is no moral failure in getting lost. But there is no gold star for staying lost, either.

Despite distractions, dead ends, and lost opportunities, a healing path exists for each of us. Everyone's healing path is available to them. But it is rarely handed to us neatly wrapped up with a bow. It is part of being human to be confused. Some spiritual people even consider confusion a higher state of consciousness. It can be a state of growing into our true selves. It is ok to be lost. It is ok to ask for help. It is ok to ask for help more than once. And there are options now that were not available in the past.

There is often an element of serendipity, synchronicity, or grace involved in finding your helpful Medicines. Because of that element of luck, it's important to read books like this one. And don't stop here. Talk to people, watch videos, walk through the world with a prayer asking to be open and aware of what, who, when, and where your helpers are. Ask for the courage to allow joy into your life.

Making collages became an important part of my path. Are you thinking "That's great for other people but I'm not talented" or "I am afraid to collage" or "I don't know how to collage, what if I do it wrong"? I assure you that with encouragement you can create strong, meaningful collages.

You are drawn to images, colors, and shapes that have meaning to you. Your inner knowingness directs you to choose one image over another and one placement over another. You choose your images and choose your placement and you glue them down. As you create, act, move your muscles, engage your listening, and spend time with yourself, the collages you produce will be unique.

This story and the ones that follow are about hope, about honoring the conflict between wanting to be our perfect selves and accepting our failure in achieving that perfection. Stories about embracing who we really are while peeling away layers of pretense and defense. Stories about finding what heals and restores us.

If we allow them, the stories will unfold and shift as we heal and grow.

Until writing this book, I held the story that dropping out of college and going back to New York was proof of my failures. I was grateful that my family would accept me even though I had crawled back.

As I wrote the words and looked at the past, I saw patterns and holes in the story for the first time – starting with how I chose which college to attend.

I visited three colleges before sending in my applications. One of my parents took me to my safety school for the interview. They were on their lunch hour, and I had to rush through the interview so they could get back to work. I visited the other two without my parents.

I chose a school that appealed to my desire to be different and inde-pendent – but that meant adding a lot of complications to my life (shopping, cooking, finding a place to live my sophomore year). The money my father promised to send each month to cover expenses stopped coming. He never explained; the money just stopped. I took a part-time job to buy groceries, laundry, and school supplies.

I am not blaming anyone. I am sharing how the story of "my years of failure" suddenly looked more like "my years of doing the best I could even as more and more issues cropped up." As I wrote, I saw it was time to remove the title of Failure and replace it with Willing to Keep Trying.

It's important as we grow and evolve to find ways to remain on good terms with ourselves. And my reliable method of keeping in touch with myself has been collage.

Collage offers an inexpensive and easily transportable way to be an artist. The materials to make collage are everywhere. They are all around us, often free. You don't even need a pair of scissors: You can rip everything up. My friend Julie asked, "Can we use our teeth to tear the paper?"

"Yes!" I answered, "There is always a way to make magic."

The biggest ongoing expense is the glue. I prefer to use glue sticks or gel medium. Some people like to use double-sided tape, double-sided foam dots and squares, spray adhesive, or white glue. If you experiment with these options you will find what you like.

Consider as well that you can also use alternative methods to adhere paper to your substrate. You can staple items down and color your staples with ink. You can sew them down by hand or with a sewing machine. You can tape them down with a decorative Washi tape from a craft shop, office supply store, or online merchant. I have even used purple safety pins to connect papers.

Not sold on purple? They are also available in many colors and sizes.

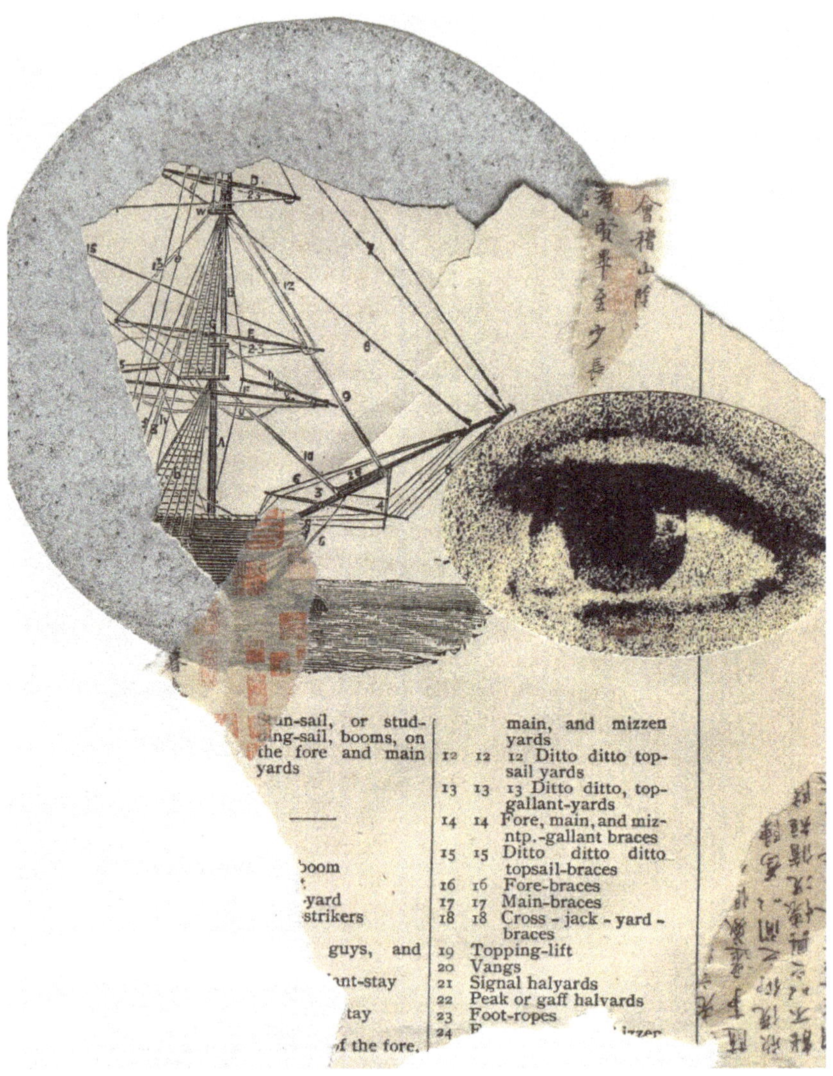

This work in progress has small torn pieces of Washi tape to hold the papers
together on the substrate.

This piece is held together with staples. The staples are intentionally placed so they become another visual element of the art. I painted the staples pink before loading them into the stapler.

You can buy elaborate papers or notebooks or scissors. But you don't have to. In the years I was couch-surfing I carried all my art supplies in a large manilla envelope. I collaged and I didn't make a mess in somebody else's house. I could make art even though I was broke or homeless or both.

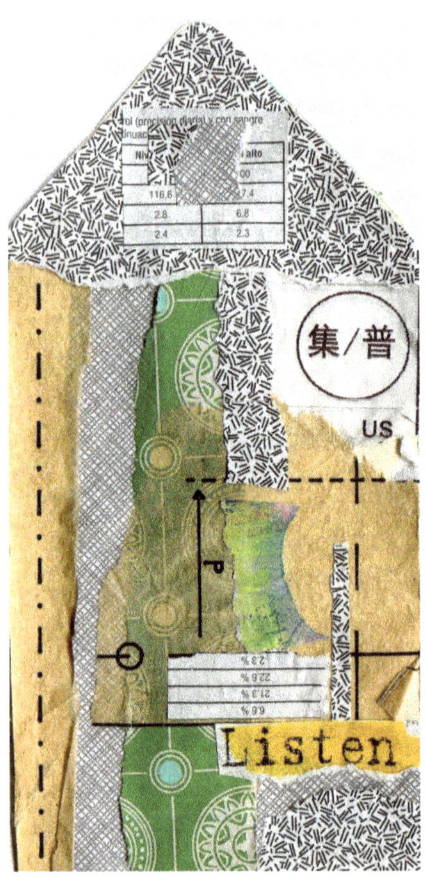

Home Again. This collage was made with papers that could be
easily found in many homes: a sewing pattern, the backs of
security envelopes that had bills in them, an insert from a
medication prescription, the front of package that was sent to me
from China, the end paper of a book, the index from another
book, and the word Listen cut out of a magazine

Following 1983, the worst year of my life, I continued to live with depression, anxiety, and periods of light mania. But I have never had another "worst year of my life." Considering what the world has recently experienced, that is saying quite a bit about how people can evolve.

Since that time, I have come back to art.

Today I introduce myself as an artist. I returned to art college and graduated with a degree Cum Laude. I'm able to hold down a full-time job. I even bought my own home — all things that in 1983 I would have told you I was incapable of doing. This shows we can be delightfully wrong about ourselves.

With all that in mind, I offer you the art and act of collage as a form of solace, of getting to know yourself. It can be a tool for communicating with yourself, for developing your intuition. Collage lets you explore the joy of color, shape, and pattern.

## Collage Call to Action

These calls to action are here to encourage you to make at least one collage after each chapter. You may find you want to make more than one collage. I hope you do.

Remember how this began? With permission to fail. So consider yourself encouraged to fail when making collages. Take the pressure off yourself. There is no need to be perfect or exceptionally good or skillful. Focus on curiosity instead. You can even write out a big sign to hang over your art-making space. Write it with your non-dominant hand. Use a bright color. Feel free to use your words. Feel free to use four-letter words. Let it appeal to the mischievous, naughty side of you.

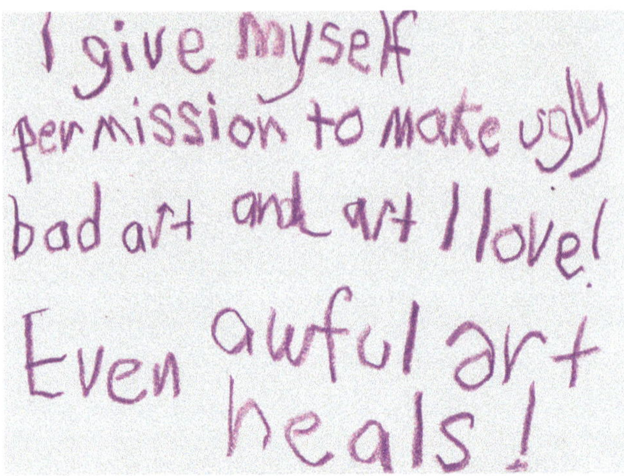


A permission slip written with my non dominant hand. A
reminder that I do not have to be perfect.

Now grab a magazine. Flip through it at a nice pace: not too fast, not too slow. If you are reading articles, you are going too slow. If you skip pages, you are going too fast. Spent about five minutes finding five or six images that catch your eye and tearing them out. You might be faster; that's great. Try not to take any longer. Remember, this is not about making a masterpiece to go into a museum. It's about warming up, dipping your toe into the collage pool, exploring something using your curiosity muscles.

Get your glue and a piece of paper that is about 8 by 10 inches. Tear the paper into four equal squares. No need to be precise. Now pick one of your images to be the focal point, the main thing that you notice when you look at your paper.

A focal point isn't always big, but for this exploration, let's go big. Find big focal points for the paper you are using as a substrate. In the collage below, the focal point is the heart - your eye is drawn to it.

Urban Heart.

Sometimes the focal point is small, as in the collage below, where we are drawn to the eyes of the face.

Remarkable

Faces have magnetic power. Babies show a preference for looking at familiar faces. Babies begin noticing faces of less familiar people at about two months. Humans continue to be drawn to faces from that point forward. This means that using a human face will usually create a focal point.

Paste your focal-point image on one of the four pieces of paper. Pick another focal point from the images you tore out of the magazine and glue that onto the next piece of paper. Continue with another focal point glued onto another piece of paper and the final focal point on the last piece of paper.

You may wonder why I asked you to choose more images than you are using. It is nice to have options, and at times that means leaving images to one side. Of course, you may decide that you want to use all the focal points you have and make more than four collages. Using the fifth and sixth focal points is valid. So is putting them aside. What's important is that you decide for yourself.

Look at what is left of the pages you tore out of the magazine. Do you find yourself drawn to a specific background or pattern? Tear those out. Find one for each of your collages. Go back to the magazine if you need to. When you have four patterns, choose one for each of your collages and paste them into place. Don't rush and don't dawdle. Adding these elements should take about five minutes.

Look at your collages for a moment. The focal point images are important, and you have added a pattern element. Now look for a word or phrase that you would like to add. Go back to the magazine to find them. When you find the words you want, tear them out. Add one or more to each collage.

Where should you add this element? It's your choice. Try holding it next to each corner of the paper. Try holding it next to other elements. If you don't find the perfect spot, put it in an OK spot.

soar.

*Hide*                    *No Persons Under 21.*

Here is one collage that illustrates three ways to use words. Which one do you think is the most interesting? Which one do you like the least? What would you change?

Go to your next collage and repeat the process. In about five more minutes, you will have four collages.

To finish the collages, get a pen and sign the front of them.

If this is your first collage, congratulations! If this is your 10,000th collage, congratulations!

# Chapter 2

## *Creating a Paper Stash*

When I was in ninth grade, I walked a dog named Homer in exchange for drawing lessons. Homer was a wiry mixed breed, built low to the ground. When he wanted to stop, there was no persuading him to move along. He'd dig in his legs and strong paws. It didn't matter if it was below 32 degrees and snowing or 100 degrees and raining. With those strong stubby legs and unbreakable willpower, he had to have been 99% Basset Hound.

Homer's human was Mrs. Journet, a musician who taught art to local ladies. She said she loved music too much to teach it to anyone.

I was extremely shy and I didn't understand how to chat with people. Something had to be done. I decided that knowing how to draw portraits would help me in social situations. Looking back, I see that it makes no logical sense to learn how to draw portraits in order to fit in better at parties. Who goes to a party with a drawing pad and charcoal, commanding people to sit still and pose for two hours?

Despite this odd logic, I did get to know two guys through Mrs. Journet – Angelo, a fellow artist who had a profound effect on my outlook on life, and Ira, my first boyfriend. (Ira fell for the oldest trick in an artist's book: He agreed to model for me – fully clothed; we were just kids.)

I visited Mrs. Journet on Saturday mornings. We sat in the small sunny room that was her home studio and she taught me how to draw faces. I made up for what I saw as my stalled artistic development with an intense focus and willingness to apply myself. I drew all the time. I was determined to draw faces that looked like the person who had modeled.

Mrs. Journet gave me a gift on my fifteenth birthday. She bought a cardboard box from the office-supply department of Woolworth's. She covered the outside with decorative paper and placed images clipped from magazines inside. She told me that all artists keep files of images. At the time, I was thrilled that she considered me an artist. Little did either of us realize what would come from this supportive present. This was the beginning of my ongoing and ever-growing paper stash. An obsession was born.

I eagerly paged through every magazine that friends and family donated to my new passion. Images filled my box in no time – so I upgraded to a larger box. Decades later, I continue to add and remove pages from my collection. I now store source materials (papers, books, magazines) in 12 transparent plastic drawers. And at any given moment there are five or six piles of paper on my art table waiting for me to choose more collage fodder.

Hunting down ephemera has been my hobby for decades. But what if you are just starting out? What can you do? Before you run out and buy subscriptions to expensive fancy magazines, read on.

## Collage Call to Action

Everyone has paper: grocery lists, to-do lists, journals, flyers from the mail, old magazines, wrapping paper, tissue paper, cocktail napkins, paper bags, paper boxes, menus from take-out restaurants. Even in the tidiest of houses you will find at least a few of these items tucked away in a junk drawer.

You might not have all of these, but you surely have some. As you look through the papers you have, begin setting aside every page that has something that appeals to you. It might be a word, a shape, a color, a texture, a person, an animal, or a flower. You don't need to know why you like it. You may not like everything on the page – maybe just a corner. That's fine. If you like it, put it in your stash. Just start gathering pages.

As you start keeping papers that appeal to you, you will notice more papers that you like. You will notice paper more often.

After you have depleted your in-house sources, add more options!

- Ask friends and family to set aside magazines and books they no longer want.
- Visit library sales, where you can pick up magazines, books, flyers, lists, and free local magazines.
- Pick up old magazines and books at thrift stores.
- Free listings on Craigslist, Facebook, and church websites.
- Coffee shops and diners often have old magazines and stacks of flyers about local events.
- Visit garage sales, flea markets, and estate sales.
- Check out used bookstores, both the brick-and-mortar version and new online stores.
- Join online collage groups, participate in collage ephemera swaps.
- Simply take a stroll. If you look hard at what is around you, you will be amazed at what you find.

If you are like me, you will be astounded by how quickly you can fill up your stash container. You will grab every image you find. You will covet every unusual example of lettering, color combination, and pattern.

Eventually you will become pickier as you realize you have more paper than any one person could use. It's a natural step along the way to defining your own process. Feel free to discard images you once thought you wanted. Feel free to hold on to papers you like even if you have no idea how you might use them.

I strongly suggest that you try the paper-finding methods and locales I've listed. One of the primary reasons is that these ideas will put your mind on the hunt. As you follow the paper trail, you become more aware of the spirit of collage. At the same time, you are alerting the universe that you are open to receiving images. You will find yourself looking at a torn envelope or a discarded handwritten note and think, "That would make a great collage." When you find that happening, you know you have entered collage flow. You have dialed into the energy wave of collage. You are looking at the world like an artist.

After a few months, you might want to branch out. You may have specific desires. You may absolutely need images of yellow cars or blue elephants. For those purposes there are unlimited options:

- Etsy
- Books entirely made of images to cut out (any bookstore will carry them)
- Art supply and craft stores
- Magazines, including free ones
- Pinterest – for free images and images to purchase
- Photo and image websites (Graphic Fairy, and more)
- Your own photos, including family photos (make color copies and save the originals)
- NY Public Library online images that are in the public domain
- Search the web for images in the public domain

You can also make your own papers. You can paint, crayon, stencil, stamp, and gel-print papers. You can copy or scan papers that you have and manipulate them in your phone's image-editing application. You can manipulate them on your computer. I often tear up old collages that don't work and reuse elements to create new pieces.

A brief word on tearing apart books for collage: I often use free books. I rarely spend more than a dollar on a book I intend to pull apart. These are not books of immense value. They are not rare books or books out of print. They are simply books that are no longer of use to the public. When we use them for collage, parts of them will go on to become art. It is a method of recycling.

There are people who feel very strongly that books should not be treated this way. If that's how you feel, exercise your artistic right to reject that source of collage papers. I encourage you to ponder whether your gut doesn't want to use books or your mind objects to pulling apart books. If it is your mind, consider where that message came from. Is it worth continuing to listen to?

And a brief word on copyright issues: If your collages are for your eyes only, copyright issues do not apply to you. If your collages are for sale, then copyright issues do apply. The laws around copyright infringement in art are not clear-cut. If you plan on using your art to mass-produce items and sell them on a large scale, it is easiest to use your own images. You can also investigate paying to use someone else's images. If you are buying images, the seller usually states at the time of sale the ways you may use their images. Often you will see the seller has a personal-use policy and a commercial-license policy. If their restrictions are not clear, you can ask them prior to using the images. If I feel uncomfortable about using an image and selling the piece, I don't sell that piece. I keep it for myself.

A quick search of the U.S. Copyright Office website turns up this information:

> *The term of copyright for a particular work depends on several factors, including whether it has been published, and, if so, the date of first publication. As a general rule, for works created after January 1, 1978, copyright protection lasts for the life of the author plus an additional 70 years. For an anonymous work, a pseudony-mous work, or a work made for hire, the copyright endures for a term of 95 years from the year of its first publication or a term of 120 years from the year of its creation, whichever expires first. For works first published prior to 1978, the term will vary depending on several factors. To determine the length of copyright protection for a particular work, consult chapter 3 of the Copyright Act (title 17 of the United States Code). More information on the term of copyright*

*can be found in Circular 15a, Duration of Copyright, and Circular 1, Copyright Basics...*

*There is no formula to ensure that a predetermined percentage or amount of a work—or specific number of words, lines, pages, copies —may be used without permission.2*

*https://www.copyright.gov/help/faq/faq-duration.html#duration*

It would be great if these rules were defined more clearly. As it is, there's a lot of gray area when using "words, lines, pages, and copies" without the creator's permission. However, we can agree that it's not cool to lift someone else's art and pretend it's ours. These reasons explain why some people opt to create all the imagery they use.

When I began making collages, the idea of selling my art was not on even the most distant horizon. I used any image from anyone and anywhere if it appealed to me. Because I thought my art would always be private, I was not concerned with copyright issues.

As it is a possibility that you may want to sell your art, I encourage you to keep notes on each piece. If you annotate the back of each collage, you will always know if the imagery is in the public domain or requires a commercial license. I would suggest the year and FS ("for sale," meaning the images were in the public domain or yours), the year and NFS ("not for sale") meaning you used images that require a commercial license to sell, or the year and FS CL, meaning you have paid the commercial license fee and can sell the art.

At one time, I would have told you that I would remember all these details without recording them. But since then, I have created thousands of collages with materials from many sources. Make it easy on yourself and make a note as you finish the piece. Years from now, you will know instantly if the piece is saleable.

You may also enjoy reading what prompted your choices or what you thought of the finished art. Did it bring you ideas for further art? Other explorations?

A paper collage with a word taken from a magazine. The circle surrounding the flower is part of a sticker, and I added some of my own handwriting with a Uni-ball Signo pen.

As you acquire more papers, you will want to keep them protected from dust, bugs, wrinkles, and other hazards. Where will you keep them? I started with the Woolworth's box and have used baskets, storage bags that zip closed, trays, envelopes, and now see-through plastic drawers.

You will also want to find a method of organizing your stash - some folks go simple with three categories:

1. Background papers
2. Focal image papers
3. Garnish and flair papers

Other people go deep with endless categories:

- Yellow in nature
- Yellow in man-made objects
- Yellow patterns
- Yellow words
- Yellow letters

Speaking of letters and words, putting those into their own containers is very popular. At one time I had a collection of Chinese fortunes in a small tin. I glued a fortune on top, which made the tin instantly recognizable. There is no right or wrong way. It's the way that works best for you.

The small tin has the fortune cookie fortune glued on top. The written word is a larger tin that has larger phrases stored inside.

One of the things I find very soothing is to take an overflowing drawer of papers and an empty drawer. I then look at all the papers and snippets one by one in the full drawer. Anything that I no longer like, I toss into a recycle bag. Things I think a friend or fellow collage artist would like I pull out to give to them. Everything else I sort through. "Let's put all the people in a new drawer. And all the patterns in a different drawer."

And I sift. I listen to music or have a movie on in the background.

Many times, while doing this, I will find papers have sort of fallen into groups in the drawer. If I have the energy, I will get my glue and glue the pages into a quick collage.

If I do not want to make a collage right away, I clip together the images so I will find them easily when I return to the drawer.

I like to use small gold binder clips. They are just big enough to grab a few papers. And the gold color catches my eye.

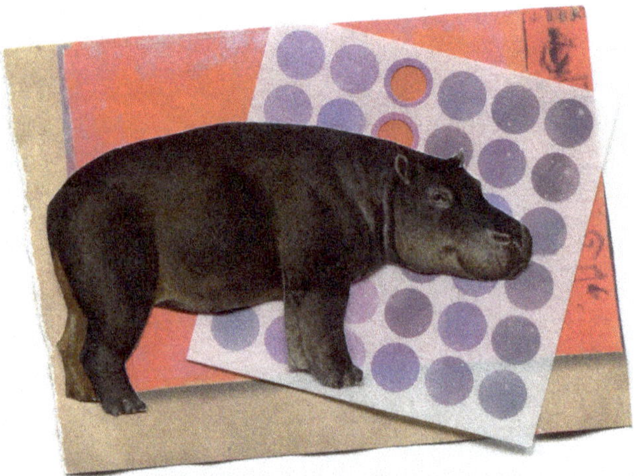

What would you put in a happy hippo collage?

But remember, the first thing is to start.

You can start with a few simple supplies and create fantastic meaningful art. You can use a simple color scheme and create a lifetime of works (see the paintings of Morandi). You can use a simple composition repeatedly and create meaningful art (see the color studies of Josef Albers). Don't fret if you are using humble materials (see the work of Kurt Schwitters).

Collecting your paper stash will be an absorbing enterprise. You may find yourself hitting up the used bookstores to find the exact copy of a book you saw someone else using. Or turning to eBay and bargaining to get a good price on a book you must own because of the amazing images of doll houses inside.

As you collect, you will notice things about your collection. "Hmm. I have tons of black-and-white pages but no orange pages at all." "I never knew I was drawn to lions and cheetahs, but look at all these photos!" Use these moments of awareness as part of your process. Notice it, honor it, hold it lightly, and use it. Let it start the conversation between you and your inner you.

Pick a way of obtaining papers and begin.

For now, look around your house for a flat chipboard box. Cereal boxes, cookie boxes, cracker boxes... these are all examples of common chipboard boxes. Take your box and peel it open. Open each end. Turn the box until you see the glue seam. Often you can peel the glued edges away. If it's not coming apart, you can cut the box open using one of the corners as a guide.

Here is a box that peeled apart easily.

You can also pull the box apart by tearing it. That works fine. You want a flat piece of cardboard on which to collage. The cardboard that you use to glue your collage onto is called the substrate. When your box is flat, turn the cardboard to the side that is not printed or not seen when you bought the box.

Here is the humble chipboard that will hold our collages.
Notice the torn edge at the top. Some people like to cut their
cardboard into precise shapes, while others like to leave them
with torn edges. Which would you prefer? Would you be
willing to try both?

Now cut or tear the cardboard into 6 x 6-inch squares. There is no need to be perfect. The substrates can be a bit smaller or larger, precise or wonky. Use a ruler to make your first square 6 x 6 inches, then use the first square as your template until you have cut or torn up all your cardboard.

Once you have your 6 x 6-inch square, look at the papers you have at hand. Pull together 9 to 12 papers from your stash. Sort them: three papers per pile. Choose three papers that are not the same but have a sympathetic comfortable feel together. If they all feel like they relate to each other, just make random choices. If none of them seem to work together, trust the process and make random choices.

Remember, you are curious and you are experimenting. You are doing quick sketches, not making the best art anyone has ever seen.

Once you have your piles, choose one to use first.

It is helpful when gluing to use an old catalog. The catalog will catch the excess glue as you run the glue stick over your ephemera element. Be sure to run the glue stick over the entire element. Then turn your paper over, place the glue side down on your substrate. You can then use your hand or a tool (small wooden block in this photo) to smooth the glued element to your substrate. This will make sure your figure is glued firmly to your background paper.

Chipboard with a first layer of decorative paper.

Take one paper to cover the bottom four inches of the chipboard. After spreading glue over your chosen paper, place it glue-side down onto your substrate. Smooth down the paper so all the edges are in contact with the cardboard. You now have a two-inch area left uncovered. Choose a paper and cover that area with glue. Then place the paper on that area, smoothing down the paper so again the two surfaces are connected.

Examples of chipboard with two layers.

You now have a covered bit of cardboard.

Let's add another piece of paper. Take your third paper and tear a smaller bit of that paper. Try letting your smaller strip tear in a slightly imperfect way. Rather than making an even stripe, try making a slightly undulating wave. Something subtly imperfect. Or if you are like me, it may be overwhelmingly imperfect – and that's OK too.

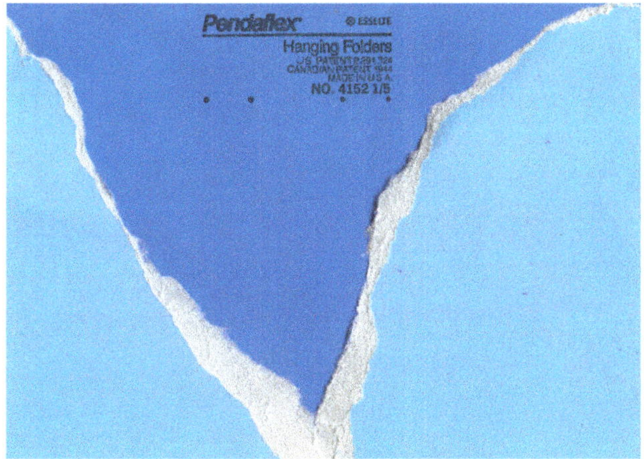

The Valley of Crumpled Pendaflex While tidying up I came
upon some old wrinkled Pendaflex folders. Tearing them was
very satisfying. The paper created a thin layer which you can
see clearly in the white shape in the upper right. Placed in
front of the darker side of the folder to reveal the tear more
starkly. Tearing paper to intentionally reveal the white inside
is a great technique for creating lines and shapes in your
collages.

You can pull the paper toward you as you tear. This will create a
white line where the core of the paper shows. Place this narrow strip
on the collage where the two earlier images meet. Try placing it so
that the bottom of the narrow strip just brushes against the upper
edge of the larger background paper. Turn the strip over and run the
glue along the paper. (Use a scrap page to lay the strip on. It will
catch the overflow glue stick, keeping your collage and work surface
free from extra glue.)

Once it is fully covered with glue, place it on your collage.

You have now created an abstract collage. Perhaps it resembles a landscape, real or imagined. Congratulations!

Does it feel like a great accomplishment? I hope so. Because this is an excellent example of how simplicity can be elegant, fun, unusual, unique, funky, different, and colorful.

Has it occurred to you that even a simple collage requires many decisions? That is one of the secrets of making art. Any time you create art, you make decisions from start to finish. The first decision sounds like "I'm going to look for some interesting colors" or "I want to play with lots of patterns" or "What happens if I use a smaller focal point?" Each decision leads you to the next choice.

Making the decisions is important. But that doesn't mean you should experience worry or anxiety. This is an opportunity to enjoy making decisions without outside interference. It is an opportunity to enjoy making art about pigs or sunflowers or Mustang convertibles for the simple reason that that is what you want to do.

It is a rare thing to be truly free to make choices. Enjoy these moments.

This collage you have made is a splendid example that shows how humble materials and simple design do not hold anyone back from creating "real" art. It is also an example of how one design can be used over and over. For example:

Use the same papers in different places.

Use a new element with previously used elements.

When you have made a few collages using these ideas, spread them out and look at them. Try turning the whole collage in different directions. Is there one orientation that feels right?

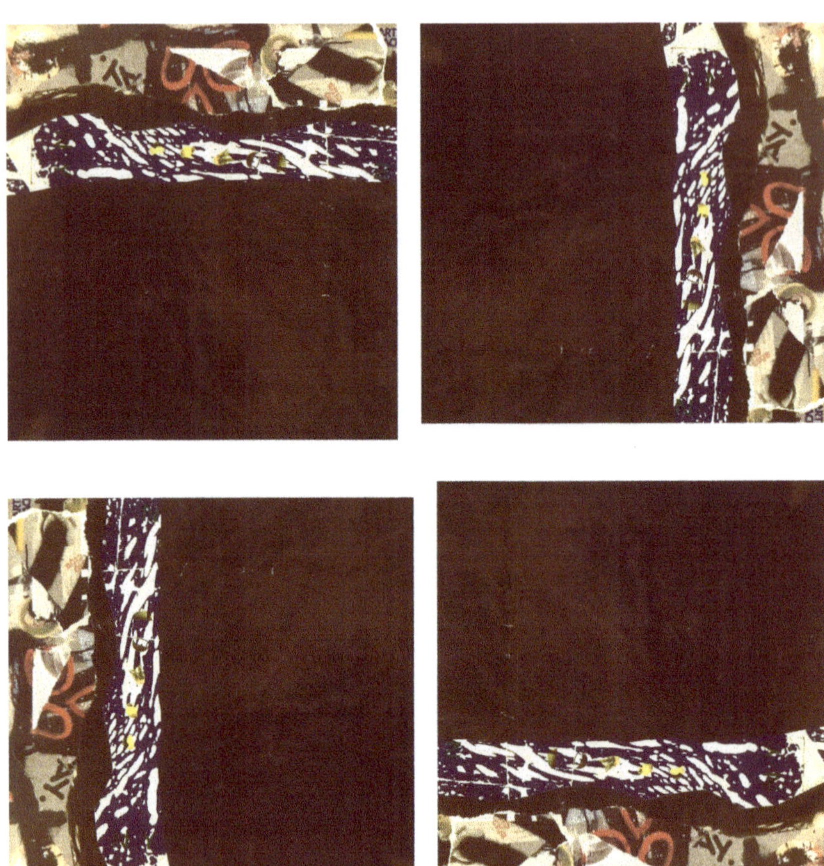

Notice how each collage is different from the others. Notice the ways they are similar. Is there one that looks more powerful? Is there one that feels more satisfying?

# Chapter 3

## *Don't Waste Your Time Being Nice*

Don't waste your time being nice. Being nice is a trap. Typically, the people telling you to be nice are using your niceness to their benefit.

Have you noticed how often the people suggesting that you should be nice will follow up with requests for you to do something for them? Have you noticed the direct correlation between how inconvenient being nice will be for you and how beneficial it will be for them to receive your niceness? How often has your gut instinct told you "Not good – exit area"?

Yet we allow the appeal to be nice to override our instincts.

I have found that depression tells us it will be easier to be agreeable. It tells us to help people in ways that oppose our self-interest.

And I have found that allowing myself to discard my self-interest darkens my mood.

Have you noticed that members of the Nice Patrol are the first to get nasty when their demands are politely and firmly turned down?

Being kind is another matter entirely. It's good for your soul and body – especially when you start by being kind to yourself. Stop being nice and start being kind.

Those of us who have been trained to be nice often default to the answer "yes."

Yes – to everyone but ourselves.

I struggled with this. I still struggle with this.

At one point, I worked with a gal who was no doubt frustrated with how saying yes to everything was affecting my work. She looked at me and said, "From now on, before you say yes, you should ask me if you are ready for more."

This agreement gave me a way of putting off requesters. "Let me sleep on it." "Let me check and get back to you."

To Amy's credit, she never said I was ready for new projects. No matter how much I argued. No matter what sad story went with the request. (It's funny how imposing requests are so often paired with heartbreaking stories.)

Having a "No thank you" partner gave me lots of practice in saying no. Eventually I was able to say no directly – including turning down work supervisors.

I remember very well the weekend that I sweated until I made the phone call declining the opportunity to overwork myself in a stressful environment with no benefit to me. As frightened as I was, as unhappy as they were, Monday came and I still had my job.

And I had a huge moment of learning what it was like to put myself first.

Saying no doesn't include taxes or caring for children and pets under your care. Once I make a commitment, I keep my promises. If that is not possible, I communicate as soon as possible that I am unable to keep my commitment. It's a horrible feeling, but it's part of being genuine. It's how you learn which yesses are good for you and which are not.

I have said "I have to say yes to them." I have heard "I have to go, I have to make that, I have to say yes." But it's rarely literally true. Rarely does it apply to the things that you've told yourself you *must* do.

I can't think of an example of something terrible happening to a person who said politely and directly, "Thank you for asking me, I am not able to participate." But I can easily recall the unhappiness that arose on occasions when everyone was saying yes contrary to their own interests.

People who say yes to everyone are saying no to everyone else. Especially themselves. Or at least, I was.

Save your yesses for yourself. Give yourself time and space to be kind. If you are new to being kind, be patient with yourself.

In the beginning of learning to be kind to myself, I called myself horrible names when I made mistakes. I know delicious salty words and I make plenty of mistakes, so there was an abundance of ugly name calling.

Once I realized how unkind it was, I vowed that there would be no more name calling – with one exception. I allowed myself to say I was a dork. It seemed friendlier and sillier than what I had been saying. Eventually, I let go of that too. If I hear myself starting to use it again, it's a clue that frustration is building up.

At first, I was deeply invested in pretending to be nice. I knew I wasn't genuinely nice. I knew I didn't understand kindness. I wasn't sure what kindness would look like.

I knew I felt caring and warmth toward my friends. That was a place to start. So, when in doubt, I'd ask myself, "How would I treat my best friend?"

If my best friend called me and said they had made a mistake at work, what would I say?

Would I say, "You are so incompetent. You are going to get fired. Everyone is talking about you"? Of course not. I would never say that to a friend.

That helped me realize it wasn't helpful or kind to say that to myself.

Eventually, the question shifted to "How does my best friend want to be treated?" and "How do I want to be treated?"

The summer I was 9, my cousin and I were going to Florida for the summer. We didn't know each other well when she arrived at my house with her suitcase.

She was immensely proud of her new bathing suit and put it on right away. "Isn't it beautiful?" she asked me. I was stunned. It wasn't beautiful. Although we were in grade school, I had an advanced aesthetic. I also had unshakeable knowledge that my aesthetic was the truth. And I took adult advice to be honest as a personal moral imperative.

The one-piece bathing suit had a thick navy blue and gold stripe. I blurted out, "You look like a bee."

She burst into tears and ran to tell my mother.

I was still trying to understand. How could she think that it was a nice bathing suit, let alone a beautiful bathing suit?

My mother came in to talk to me. My mother told me my cousin's feelings were hurt.

I was confused. Wouldn't it hurt her feelings even more to go out in public and *then* find out she looked terrible? Wouldn't it hurt my feelings to deny my superior knowledge of beauty? When did lying become the best policy? Why was my cousin not only a misguided fashion wannabe but also a crybaby and a tattletale?

I was stubborn and opinionated. My mother and I went around and around. Finally we agreed that I would say I was sorry. By that point, I was indeed sorry. I was sorry she had ever shown me her stupid bathing suit.

The fashion critic (left) and the cousin who I declared looked
like a bee (right). I am carrying a lot of baggage already.

Being told to be nice is like offering weak tea to someone who needs antivenom. If someone had explained why it is important to be kind, it would have been more helpful for my cousin and me. That didn't happen. I apologized as nice girls do, but I was no closer to being kind.

Years later, I grew increasingly skeptical of the oppression of women. As a young female artist, it was obvious that museums were filled with art made by men. All the women I knew were responsible for birth control. At my office, women assisted their male superiors. The very few women who were promoted were not respected. They were denigrated by the men, accused of being tokens or whores or ball-busters.

I was proud of understanding the "truth." Then the day came when I heard myself making snarky comments about the wardrobe of a female VP who was introducing speakers at a work event. Suddenly I understood that to be a true supporter of women I would have to accept their right to dress how they wanted. Without judgment. Without snide commentary. *Sigh.*

I was disappointed in myself for buying into the shame game. At the same time, I was sad to give up the game.

I did know that allowing myself to feel how I feel is an enormous kindness. It was healthier for me to admit to myself that I did not like what she was wearing – and support her right to wear it – than to pretend I did like it.

Admitting that you are depressed or ill or burned-out or angry or hurt is more healing and supportive than any elaborate pretense of nice-ness can ever be. It means eating when hungry, drinking when thirsty, resting when tired, and saying I'm sorry when I am.

Being honest with yourself about your real feelings is a form of Medi-cine. It is never a license to lash out at people. Not even yourself.

Being kind means trying again when something is important to you. And it means letting yourself really suck at something that you are trying for the first time. Or the 50th time. It's kindness to offer ourselves grace when we see it's time to evolve and learn.

## Collage Call to Action

Kindness can take many forms. Out of curiosity, I have asked people what kind things they have done for other people. I am amazed how often the question leaves people speechless. If I know the person, I can make a list for them. I notice when people are kind.

When I mention all the things I remember, the usual response is "Oh that, that wasn't a big deal." But we can't always know what was a big deal to the recipient.

After my father died, I ran into one of his neighbors. This neighbor had been a young child when we moved into the apartment building. He had always been shy, not one to say much. He had a slight neurological issue that was not well understood at the time.

He surprised me when he offered condolences and then told me, "Your father was a very nice man. He's the only person in the building who ever said hello to me."

I was sad to hear that none of the other adults had acknowledged him. I was also touched that my father's hello had been a kindness that this man had carried with him all his life. It is unlikely that my father thought of it as one of his great acts of kindness.

This exchange got me thinking about how I wanted to be in the world.

Think for a bit about all the ways that you have offered kindness to yourself and to others.

Let's create a collage that represents the kindness you have given to the world. Let's use images and colors that express your experiences.

For this experiment, let's not use words. Consider what images bring to mind your kind spirit. What colors make you feel soothed? Or make you smile? What shapes make you feel peaceful and calm?

Feel those emotions as you look through your papers. Pull out all the images and papers you find that make you feel lighthearted.

If you have a photo of yourself, make a copy. Place the image of yourself in the middle of a large paper (poster board or a paper bag – any large paper will be fine). If you have other photos of yourself where you are having fun or being kind, you can use those as well.

With your image on the page, begin placing images around you. Continue until you reach the outer edges of your paper. When you are done, you will have a field of the kindness that you have sent out to the world.

This collage has a copy of a painting (representing the art I have given to friends), a dragonfly (representing a pin I gave an artist I admire), a mannequin (representing the one I found tossed out on a New York City street, which I dragged through the city to the commuter train and then blocks on the sidewalk to give to my sister for her birthday), people on the beach (representing a vacation I gave to my mother), a pen (representing all the "thank you" letters I have written for people who go above and beyond) and a map (representing a trip I gave my father to visit his sister). Remember that only you must understand what the images mean. This collage is to remind you how much you have given to yourself and the people around you.

It is empowering to realize how much we have done and are able to do, even as we struggle with negative self-talk and dark moods. It is important to remember we are more than our difficult days. Every kindness we can offer improves our ability to live with kindness toward ourselves. Admire the tender force you can be.

# Chapter 4

## *Lost Time*

At seven, I kept a diary.

The first entry: "I am sick."

The second entry: "I am still sick."

The third entry: "I hate being sick."

Measles and mumps had spread through my family. They recovered while I developed strep throat and lingering neck spasms.

I lost time to that long series of illnesses. I left school as a physically active kid who was going to participate in the school Olympics and returned in a neck cushion. I've never enjoyed competitive sports since.

As a child, I had chronic ear infections and chronic strep throat. As an adult, I've had mood swings and chronic depression. Luckily, I was generally able to work and earn money. But there were hours, days, weeks lost to the heavy wet malaise of depression.

Sometimes in the useless game of "what if," I try to follow the threads back to a place in my past where I could have altered the course of my life. "What if I had found a Jungian therapist in college, would I have gotten better faster?" "What if I had been able to focus on having a career earlier, would I have been happier?"

Every time, I conclude that there really wasn't one crossroad that would have led to a prettier, more traditional, more logical life.

It is amazingly easy to use all the time lost to depression to spiral deeper into another episode. I have found trying to find the "wrong turn" or the "wrong choice" leads to more time lost, more time spent in the mire of being depressed. Although acknowledging and grieving the lost years, months, or days is an expression of genuine feelings, climbing into that grief and staying there is not good Medicine.

If someone who is struggling with depression, anxiety, or bipolar disorder were to ask me for advice I would mention these things:

1. Don't kill yourself.
2. Keep trying things until you find what works.
3. No one thing works all the time for everyone. Meds, spiritual practices, exercise, diet, prayer, energy work, primal scream... each is the answer or part of the answer for some people. People cling to their favorites: "It's great," they say. "It healed me." It healed them or maybe it didn't. Either way, it may or may not be your path. It could be your path, but only for a while. That's OK.
4. Put yourself in the company of kind people. Spend time with people who are interested in evolving. The world is too impressed with important, rich, powerful people. This is a con. Don't fall for it.
5. Keep to a schedule as much as you can: waking up, eating, going to sleep.

6. Gather all your good moments. They may be just seconds here and there, but they are yours. Gather them and keep them. Keep photos or lists or talismans as tangible reminders.

7. During a "bad patch" or "flare up" or extreme stress, be tender with yourself. Be loving when you are unable to stay on top of schedules, good moments, friendships. Reread #1 - life isn't always pretty, but *stay here.* The worst weather will pass.

8. No matter how bad you feel, continue to offer your gifts to the world.

## Collage Call to Action

Even when I was a broke, unemployed couch surfer, I was still able to make collages. I could give collage cards I had made to people. Back then, you could often find free postcards in diners, clubs, galleries, and other places. I scooped them up whenever I saw them. Then I took them home and altered them.

I added fish to a cityscape or a huge butterfly to a river scene. I drew with markers and pens. I added zany words or patterns.

Once I was satisfied with the added flourishes, I wrote a note to a friend or family member and mailed it off.

Why is it so important to continue to offer your gifts to the world? Because depression lies to us. It whispers, "You are nothing. You have nothing. You will always feel this way." Depression sometimes uses more elaborate ways to tell you these things, but it always wants you to believe you will fail.

Creating a collage and sending it to a friend is sending a strong message to those voices. The message is "I am worthy, I do matter. I have an abundance of care and creativity that I share with others. I will continue. I will feel differently soon." It is an act of defiance. It is an act of choosing yourself over the darkness.

Do you have a postcard that you can alter? If not, you can cut up a cereal box into 3 x 4-inch rectangles. Fill one side with images of bright colorful fruit or insects or planets. Find fun words to use on the back. "Welcome! Laugh! You are loved! The Best! Sing! I love you as much as these planets! Orange you glad I sent you this card?"

Sign your name. Put their address on the right side of the card, add a stamp, and mail it away. People always prefer your perfectly imperfect postcard over the perfect card that you never mailed. Everyone loves mail. You can spark that happy feeling with your creativity, glue, and a stamp.

Sometimes, when I'm feeling stuck, I say, "I'm just going to do one." By the time I've created a postcard, I often have ideas and want to make more.

If you find yourself in that space, go for it.

Other times, I have images and words that go together but I don't have the time to make more postcards. Using a binder clip, I put the bits that go together into a bundle for future use.

Once I got a great letter from a friend. After reading it, I thought, I'm going to send the best card.

Because it had to be the best, I wasn't able to create anything good enough. I resorted to looking in shops for the perfect card.

One day I realized six months had passed while I was looking for the perfect card. I sat down and wrote an ordinary note on ordinary note paper.

Later, they asked why I hadn't been in touch for six months.

Don't be a perfectionist. People want to hear from the real you. Waiting to be perfect, letting months go by, leaves a weird space for everyone to start making up stories about what's going on. Don't make weird silent spaces. Make art.

These collages were made using postcards as the substrate. You can see small areas of the original cards peeking out. I added elements on top until I was happy with the result. It would be great fun to send altered cards to a penpal, encouraging them to return the favor.

Old school yearbooks are full of photos of groups of students. Often, they have marvelous and unexpected expressions on their faces.

# Chapter 5

## *When the going gets tough, give up*

Give up? Really?

How often are we told to work harder? To try again? How often do we try harder when the going gets tough?

Have you ever found yourself in a situation that got worse and worse as you fought against it?

I have been in situations where no matter how much I thought, plotted, strategized, acted, and reacted, everything just went downhill faster. The more I resisted, the greater the pressure grew.

These are the times when the best response is to give up. To surrender. Just lie down on the ground and say, "OK, I give up."

Once I came upon a neighbor while I was walking my dog. As we chatted, she mentioned that she had been rushed to the hospital from work. I asked if she was OK, and she laughed. "In the ambulance, I realized it was a chance to rest," she said.

Her life had gotten so stressful she had reached the point of surrender in the ambulance. She was lying on the stretcher and decided to take it as a chance to rest. She recognized a good moment to surrender.

## Collage Call to Action

Find a magazine, preferably an exotic one full of unfamiliar images and words in a foreign language.

Grab a glue stick and look through the magazine.

Remember not to read the articles. Turn the pages slowly enough to see the images but quickly enough so you aren't skimming the text or poring over details.

As you see a color, pattern, or image that grabs your interest, tear out the page.

When you've gone through the magazine, put it aside. Look at the pages you tore out.

Which elements do you like the most? Which do you like the least?

Tear away what is unnecessary from your favorite page.

Pull out four or five more images from your pile. Tear out the parts that are meaningful to you.

Take your torn pieces and arrange them on your substrate. Imagine that the torn pages are messages from the part of you that uses images to talk. As adults we have given the word-using part of our personality endless hours to talk. Often, we turn to words first when we are in a pickle. It's as if we have an inner filibuster with language refusing to yield the floor.

Ironically, that wordy part of us often isn't saying anything nice or kind or useful to us. The word spewer is connected to the part of ourselves that is obsessed with keeping us safe, keeping us in a linear, logical, physical system.

There is another part of us that uses images to communicate. The image user is thrilled to have a chance to tell its story.

When you first allow it to speak up, it can be very shy. It hasn't had the years of practice that the verbal part has had in learning how to capture your attention.

Yet the image maker has many things to say. And the longer it has been waiting for a chance to commune with us, the more it has to tell us.

At first, the images tumble out with no discernable pattern. They can seem contradictory, simultaneously too simple and too complex.

Don't worry. The more often you check in, the easier it will become.

In those early conversations, try not to grab or grasp. Don't force anything.

(That's why I mostly use the words "play" and "experiment" in this book. I'm avoiding using the word "work" for creative exploration. Life is already too worky.)

I've seen collages tell secrets and stories. And yet it's not to be taken too seriously. Respectfully, yes. Seriously, tensely, anxiously? No.

I've seen collages created in five minutes. And if you've ever created something in that amount of time, you know you don't have enough time to analyze everything. But the image maker and the collage maker collaborate to find the perfect photo.

We see a woman in the foreground and a hand plugging cables into her where her heart is. I made this collage sitting at the kitchen table of an apartment in Jersey City. I was cat-sitting for the owner. After work, I returned to his apartment and spent hours making collages.

I had a new job and was living in a new place. Without conscious thought, my image maker was expressing my willingness to open my heart up to new experiences. Its message jumps out at me today. But at the time, I was focused on the colors and shapes.

Experiences like this have taught me to be patient. To listen to my inner whisperings and to trust that making the piece is meaningful, even when my conscious brain is unaware of what it all means.

It was only years later that I realized I made that one just a few weeks before I began dating a new guy.

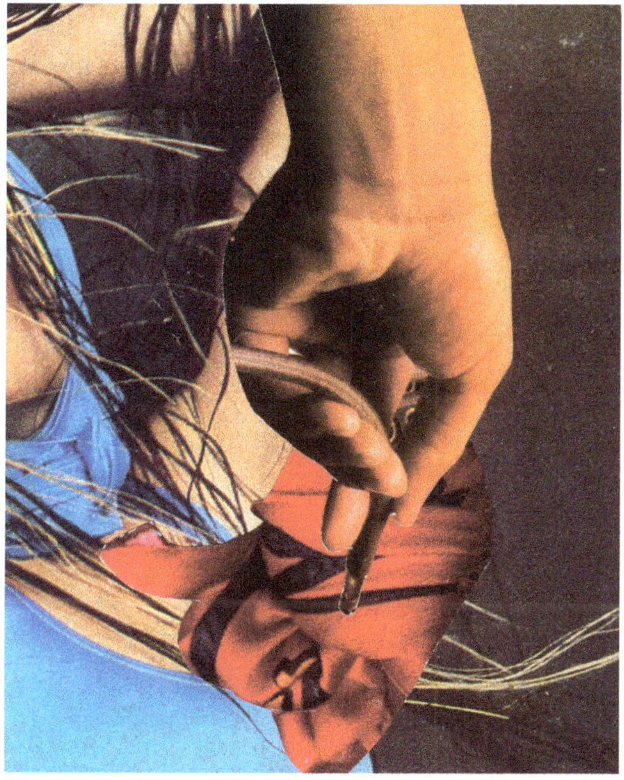

Switching on the Heart. This collage shows a woman in the background and a shape that is reminiscent of a heart. On top of the heart-like shape is a hand with a switchboard plug.

So you have the images you've chosen. Arrange them without excess thought. Try putting small shapes next to bigger ones. Try putting dark shapes next to bright ones. Try putting a neutral color next to a wild pattern. Try turning your substrate upside down or left or right. Add an element while your collage is upside down. Glue down your choices. Write on the back: "My Story Number 1."

Then take another substrate and repeat the process with your next five images. But this time create a new message with assorted colors and shapes. Try to decide and glue down four or five torn bits in about 15 minutes.

Imagine these are short messages in a foreign language that you are learning. Trust that you will understand the language and the messages in time. Enjoy the process of helping your non-verbal side send these statements.

Make at least two more. Remember to name them and number them. "My Story Number 2." "My Story Number 3." "My Story Number 4."

Put them aside for now. If four seems like too many, repeat the design of your first one three times.

Here are some examples:

Example: Butterfly One with Lotus Lady

Example: Butterfly 6

Example: Wisdom

# Chapter 6

## *Missing People*

A Missing Man filled with shattered glass.

Of all the people who have gone missing, I'm going to miss me most of all.

This thought crossed my mind as I started this chapter.

If you are ever tempted to remove yourself from your life, hopefully you will be lucky enough to have a friend like Angelo.

I caught my first glimpse of him outside Mrs. Journet's apartment. I was leaving after walking Homer one evening when a young man practically knocked me over as he ran into her apartment. Although it was dark and he was little more than a blur, I saw enough to realize he was extraordinarily good looking.

I glimpsed him three or four more times before we met. I had stopped by Mrs. Journet's classroom, I remember. It was a large space with generous windows that let in sunlight for the students. The walls and floor were all painted a mid-tone gray that didn't interfere with color choices in paintings the students were creating.

My mother was in the class, and I had to pick up a key. But all thoughts of keys and locks abandoned my consciousness when Angelo rushed into the room.

The class was a congenial group of women of various ages. I could see that the ladies were fond of Angelo. They called out greetings and questions. "How is your painting coming?" "Congratulations on winning the Guild award." He answered politely and conducted his business with Mrs. Journet.

She then introduced us, pointing out that we were fellow artists. He smiled and asked if I wanted to go with him to the public library to pick up an entry form for an upcoming art show.

All the ladies encouraged me to go. He raced out of the studio and down the stairs. I ran to keep up. Angelo was always in a hurry, always rushing to start and finish a painting or rushing to work to earn money so he could buy more paint.

Angelo was the most handsome person who had ever spoken to me. I have always had a weakness for beauty. I was always slightly stunned by him. With his thick, dark curly hair and his strong chin, he looked like Michelangelo's David come to life.

We spent a lot of time together that summer. We drew together. He painted and we talked. We went to the movies. We went out for pizza or sandwiches.

Shy and insecure, I wanted to be talented but doubted that I was. I had given up dreams of being swept off my feet by a kind, handsome guy. But as we spent time together, I gradually began to believe anything might be possible. This amazing fellow believed in me.

My father was extremely critical of everyone. He shared his opinions readily and frequently with his family. His children were not going to be caught by surprise out in the world. We were all aware of our shortcomings.

Angelo never criticized me or my art. Like a neglected houseplant, I grew toward his sunny, affectionate friendship. We looked forward to being in the same progressive high school. We would be able to spend most of our days in the art studio.

But it was not to be. One afternoon in late August, he stopped by my family's apartment to talk to me. His mother had kicked him out of the house. He had moved into a friend's place in Manhattan.

I was confused. Clearly something was very wrong, but he seemed calm.

I said, "I don't understand." He sighed.

"I told her I was gay," he said. "And she told me to get out."

I didn't know what to say. I couldn't imagine how he would manage. He was used to being surrounded by sisters and cousins and aunts and grandmothers. How would he adapt to life without them? How would he earn a living and survive?

I was worried about him. But I was also a sheltered person with lots of rigid, narrow-minded ideas. After he left, I grappled with the obvious and enormous disconnect between my experience of Angelo and the stories I had heard about homosexuals.

I tried to cling to teachings of right and wrong that had been presented to me as divine truth. But they could not stand up to my experience of Angelo. He was a young person who loved people. He was talented, encouraging, kind, and caring. He wanted to be swept off his feet just like I did. How could any of that be wrong? He had never been evil, bad, defective, or cruel.

I did not consider myself a rigorous intellectual or a deep philosopher. I was not a member of good standing in the religion of my ancestors, having been invited to leave religious instruction and never come back. After an intense and unexpected internal search for the truth, I made my decision. One Angelo was worth every religious bigot I'd ever met.

My worldview cracked open just enough to let in some light. Having chosen friendship over dogma, I began to worry even more about his circumstances.

He grew up very quickly. He invited me to meet him at the private club where he tended bar. Looking impossibly more handsome than ever, he would take me to dinner and dancing.

When there was no cash, he painted on cardboard instead of canvas. We sat and drank cheap beer as we talked about the art we were creating.

I knew things were not easy for him. I knew he was heartbroken by his mother's rejection. I felt helpless.

When I was accepted into art school, he was happy for me. A true friend, he wanted me to be happy, to do my art and to be treated well.

Whenever I returned home for a visit, we always met and caught up. If he was able to borrow a car, he'd pick me up and we would drive to New York City. We cranked up the music and I felt the wind in my hair, the two of us dressed up for an evening in a club. When I told him about people who didn't treat me well, he reminded me that I deserved better. I loved spending time with him.

One night he was very sad. He brought up his looks for the first and last time. "I never know if I am loved for me or for my beauty," he said. Until that moment, I had no idea how he saw himself or how lonely he felt. His features were not flawless. He looked like an actual human. But he was gorgeous, and his heart was open, which drew people to him.

After high school and my years in Philadelphia, I returned to New Rochelle for a two-week visit in 1980. My stay lasted much longer than two weeks. I ran out of money, so I took jobs working in the coffee shops along North Avenue and Main Street. I told myself it was just to make pocket money until I returned to Philadelphia.

I remember visiting Angelo in his art studio one day after my lunch shift and before his dinner shift. It was a single large room, the walls and floor painted gray. A mattress lay near an easel with a hot plate and coffee pot on a small shelf he had hung up. The building wasn't zoned for residential use. It had no hot water, and the toilet and sink were in the hallway. If the landlord suspected Angelo was living there, he looked the other way.

Angelo showed me the portraits he was painting for an upcoming show. I thought he was incredibly talented. Painting seemed effortless for him. And he always knew what to say to people. He was confident.

I was still dazzled by his chiseled features and his ferocious passion for painting. He had over time convinced me that we were peers. He had been supportive of my going to college to study art. He had never shown any envy, even as he struggled to survive in New York City.

Now I was back in our hometown. Waitressing.

I was a spectacularly awful waitress. When customers waved me down to ask where their food was, I just stared at them blankly. I had no recollection of speaking to them before.

After I admired the portraits he was painting, Angelo invited me to come back on my next day off and draw with him.

"No thanks," I said. "I've given away all my supplies. I'm not an artist." I had dropped out of college, I explained. I was not an artist, but an awful waitress.

I had glossed over what had happened to bring me back to New Rochelle. I wasn't being secretive; I didn't understand it myself. At the time, I just knew I had to move away from the pain of being called an artist. Being an awful waitress was much easier.

Angelo grabbed my arm. "Yes, you are! You are an artist."

He was insistent that we draw together – not just that day, but every time we met. He wouldn't accept my erroneous self-assessment. He knew I was an artist. He wouldn't pretend that he agreed with me.

Instead of making a life plan, I learned to type and took temp office work. Eventually, my two-week visit to New Rochelle had lasted longer than the entire time I had lived in Pennsylvania. I still hadn't really chosen to stay in New York. I was just drifting.

I worked and I took night classes at the local community college. I didn't have a car, so I took buses everywhere. This schedule accounted for all my time. Being busy was and still is a popular and socially acceptable way of avoiding pain.

Inner Space

Being busy also makes it possible to avoid people who call you out on how you are hiding from yourself. After a time, Angelo and I rarely saw each other.

And then he resurfaced. He'd had a breakdown and the cops had called his father. He was living at home again. He told me his mother had died very quickly of cancer when he was living in New York City. His sisters were happy to have him at home. He and his father were getting along.

He looked well. He told me that he had always dreamt that he and I would end up getting married and live in his childhood home. This was as realistic as anything I had heard from straight guys I had dated. We were both a bit pummeled by life and people. It was reassuring to be calm together even though we both knew we were not going to marry.

Shortly after this he stood me up. I was going to pick him up from his job and drive him home. We'd do art and talk. Eat leftovers or get pizza. One of his co-workers told me Angelo had gone home an hour early. I was embarrassed, hurt, and angry.

We didn't speak again. I told myself I was busy. I told myself he would walk across town, appear at my door, and we'd catch up like nothing had happened. Or he'd call and ask me to meet him for lunch.

Instead, a student of Mrs. Journet's gave my mother the news. He had died. He was gone at 27 years old. No one said AIDS. It was New York in the 1980s. Everyone knew.

His sisters were organizing a show of his portraits. I went to the library to see the whole show before it came down.

My portrait was painted by Angelo.

He had always focused on faces, especially eyes. Isn't that where you first see that someone loves you? You see their eyes light up when they look at you. And isn't that where you look to reassure yourself you are still loved? Are their eyes bright and sparkling when they see you? Or do they go flat?

I couldn't believe he was gone. I had assumed we would have decades together. I was wrong.

Years later, I know how rare such friendship is. Only now do I understand that people do not always recover from heartbreak and rough living. The rosy cheeks and sparkle in their eyes can be a fever as easily as it can be restored health. Now I understand that he clung to the dream of living in his family home as a safe place he could always return to.

I know now how illness can make you forget plans. How it can leave you without the energy to spend time with a close friend. I forgive him for standing me up and I forgive myself for losing the last year we could have spent as friends.

Bethesda Fountain in Central Park, New York City.
Watercolor by Angelo.

Now I understand that shutting the door on my identity as an artist after going to art school is ironic. But over the years, I have recognized that there were many things besides art school that led me to giving up on art.

Maybe you will relate to some of these factors.

- I was not expecting the intensity of so many artists in one space.
- I had supportive teachers and friends in high school. It was very different in college, where jealousy, competition,

attention-seeking, hormones, fear, and anxiety led many students to be mean.

- I was unable to imagine any way of supporting myself as an artist.
- One day I thought I had real talent, the next day I was sure I was deluding myself.
- I was unprepared when the college changed the curriculum from a single major to requiring all students to have a double major. I wanted to study weaving, not pottery or jewelry making.
- I lost my family's financial support suddenly, without explanation.
- I had to work part-time to make money for food, laundry, and art supplies.
- The non-traditional campus meant no food plan. And I had to find a place to live after freshman year.
- I had an undiagnosed yet deeply felt mood disorder.
- I lacked a support team.
- I received mixed family messages: Be a superstar, but don't ask for help.
- I didn't know how to cook, shop for food, or organize my time .
- I bluffed my way through life rather than asking questions.
- I rushed into life before I was ready, before I asked myself what I wanted. Before I had a chance to process one experience, I had thrown myself into the next. I wasn't learning from the last fiasco; I was stacking them up.

I was doing the best I could. If I'd had the luxury of wise counsel, I might have been encouraged to wonder why I was attracted to a school where many of the students were crying on the school tours for potential students. (I thought it was proof of how passionate and romantic they were.)

A traditional campus would have been better for me. The structure would have allowed me to focus on my studies. Instead, I drifted into situations that siphoned off time and energy.

I was lucky, until college, to have teachers who were pleased by their students' talent and success. It was a shock to feel the sting of cruel comments that jealous college art teachers made. And it seemed to me that most of the people who enrolled as students were more interested in living out stereotypes of the artistic life with none of the substance.

My estrangement from art has a happy ending.

One day I randomly found myself in a student show at the NY School of Visual Arts. As I walked through the gallery, a great sadness and longing filled me.

It felt as if I had run into a long-lost love. I yearned to reclaim the affection and the love I had had in the past with art, my true love. I no longer remembered what drove us apart. All I wanted was to be back in their arms.

I walked out of the gallery. I cautiously welcomed myself back into my heart and back into my life. I was lost, but now I was found.

And I knew myself to be an artist.

Gradually I put my life back on track. With therapy, I eventually learned that other people's opinions of me are none of my business. I learned that other people's poor behavior is about them. Knowing that, it can still sting even now.

I have learned that having talent matters much less than having passion and curiosity. One of my teachers once mentioned that five years after leaving art school, fewer than 10% of students are still making art. It surprised me at the time, but I have seen that it is true. Two of my most creative friends stunned me by giving up art. But they chose other paths. I think their experiences in art school helped them choose what felt authentic to them as they moved through life.

During the time I went missing. I looked like myself on the outside. But inside I was AWOL. I had rejected and removed art from my life. In its place I put chunks of drama and chaos, staying up late, working hard.

Cramming things inside of ourselves that aren't true is painful. And being busy and tired is one way of distracting from that pain.

## Collage Call to Action

Here's an exercise for Missing People.

Find a photo of yourself or someone else who is missing. Make a few color copies of them. Make sure the image is large enough person for you to place other images inside the figure. Cut the person out of the photographs, being careful to keep the photo of you intact and the background intact. You will have two pieces – you and everything else.

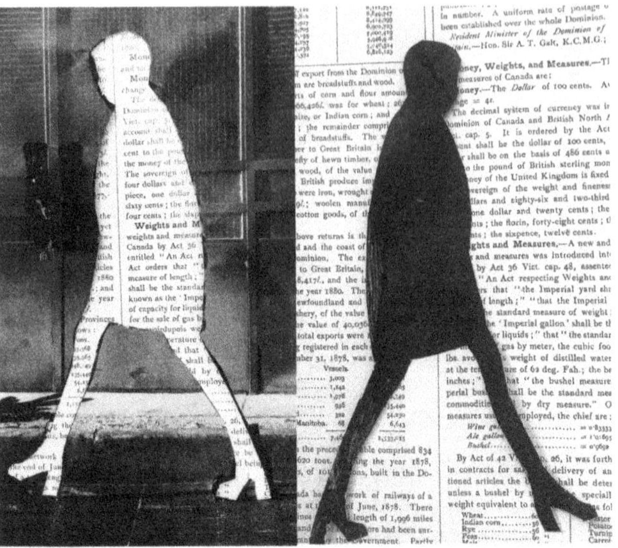

Image on the left was left after the figure was cut out. Image
on the right is the back of the figure placed on a background
of text.

Look through your stash of papers. Pull out papers that express your
experience of what filled the empty space.

This exercise can easily be altered - you can use a current photo of
yourself, for example, and fill your inner space with images that
reflect your aspirations.

You can use another photo of yourself from a time in your past - and
fill the inner space with images from the extraordinary life you
thought you would lead – even though everyone else thought you
were an ordinary fourth grader.

Sometimes we miss other people who have removed themselves. You
can fill their void with images and colors that reflect your loss. Or you
can fill the void with images that reflect what their healing will be.

Maybe you miss the relationship you had together. You can fill your
void with what would have given you peace. You can fill their void

with what would have given them peace. You can use missing people's collages in so many ways. This is a form of Medicine that can support the real you, that can give you peace and forgiveness.

A missing man filled with well used tools.

# Chapter 7

## *Black Crows*

The freshman drawing teacher had us drawing in the dark. We spent hours making marks with ink and all kinds of tools, experimenting with putting ink onto newsprint. He introduced exercises and ideas I had not been exposed to before. He sent us off to create a self-portrait over a holiday break. My roommate helped me by taking a photograph that I could draw from. I put a lot of effort into the portrait. I returned to class, confident that I'd get praise, a small suggestion for improvement and a bit more praise.

Instead, the teacher turned to the class and said "The drawing is fine, there's nothing wrong with it. But isn't the whole thing trite?" Then he sighed a deep sigh to convey exhaustion. Exhaustion brought on from having to look at such unoriginal and stale work. He continued to talk. No doubt begging everyone else not to torture him with such pathetic mediocrity.

But I have no idea because I went into shock and shame. The moment the critique was over, I fled the class and hid in my dorm room. Hours later I returned to retrieve my supplies and the work of shame. Sadly, the wooden box that had all my drawing supplies was gone. Some creep had added injury to my insult and helped themselves to that nice box filled with charcoal, pencils, sharpener, and erasers.

At the next class, I told the teacher my supplies were stolen and I'd replace them when I got paid. The class after that I showed up with a metal fishing box with pencils. At the end of class that day, I had managed to draw nothing. The class after that I told him I wasn't able to draw. I had shoved the shock and shame inside. I was able to say honestly, I don't know why I'm not able to draw.

Maybe he realized he had something to do with my sudden inability to move my hand across paper with a pen or pencil. After telling me to do what I could, he left me alone for the rest of the semester. He gave me a passing grade. Maybe he was more careful with students after that year.

Years later in another state and another college, I was drawing in a non-credit continuing education class. My version of the still life we were working on was awkward and stiff. But I was enjoying myself. The teacher was supportive of all of us scraping graphite onto 18 x 24 paper. She had a pair of simple jade earrings that she wore every time I saw her. It struck me as a symbol of her nature. She was unlikely to change how she talked to the class from week to week.

One night, she stopped at my spot "Surgeon or artist? Your parents" she asked.

"Artist, my mother" I answered. My mother was artistic, studied painting, eventually got a degree in photography.

"It's always one or the other when I see this talent," she pointed to my page. From that moment on she became a self-appointed noodge. She insisted I return to college and get my art degree. She offered to write a letter on my behalf to the dean of students.

We were sitting on a cement bench outside the classroom during a break. "All you have to do is get that piece of paper." She encouraged me relentlessly. For months. Until I agreed.

Oracle

I enrolled but I refused to chase that piece of paper. Instead, I planned to enjoy myself. I liked her class, but I had no plans on drawing as an enrolled college student.

Despite my promise to myself, I discovered that I was required to take a class in drawing.

In this class taught by another teacher, I managed to draw so lightly that you would have been within your rights to ask if there were any pencil marks on the paper. If the drawings were mostly invisible, how much trouble could I get into? My drawings were the visual equivalent of whispering.

We had one assignment which involved drawing boxes on top of each other with lines to represent a two-point perspective. I had managed to grit my teeth and whisper my way through every other assignment in that class that semester. However, those lines representing imaginary perspectives overwhelmed me.

I ran out of class that day crying. No fear, I had learned to take my supplies with me and not to keep anything expensive at school. At the apartment, my friends huddled around me supportively. First everyone agreed the teacher was a heartless witch. Then we all agreed that I was doing really well, this was just a bit of a flashback. Did I want them to walk with me to the next class? No? Would I like them to wait outside the classroom to walk me home when it was over? No? Then when I got home, how about a warm mug of hot tea and a snack. That sounded rather good.

With all that support, I managed to finish the assignment and brought it to the next class. She never mentioned my abrupt departure. Just as she never asked me why my drawings were so faint. I passed the class. I was free to never draw again.

My intention to enjoy myself informed my choices in things large and small. I read the class listings each semester and ran to sign up. Then, assured of my spots in Japanese Film, Yoga, Woodworking, Art in The Dark, I would sign up for an appointment with my advisor. He was a nice man, a printmaker whose name you might recognize but to protect everyone let's not worry about his name.

He would look over my choices carefully. After nodding at them, he'd say "It's strange, I don't remember discussing these classes with you earlier." Which was the order in which students were told to register each semester. I had discovered the problem with that process was that many classes would be full by the time you got to talk with your advisor. Each time, I would respond "Hmmm" to convey how odd that was without actually giving anything away. With a twinkle in his eye, he would sign off on my choices.

At the end of each semester, I would wander the art studios and peek into various classes. If people were laughing or smiling I put the class on my list. One of these was a class taught by a nice laid back guy. I mentioned to one of my friends that I was going to take one of his classes. "Oh, he's interesting. He's a musician and he has adopted a village in Peru. He visits them once a year." He was also a photographer, filmmaker and visual artist.

During class he once referred to a series of drawings I had done as a nice quartet. But that was the only musical reference he made. He was focused on our drawing. He sent us outside in all kinds of weather to draw, he sent us to the museum on campus to draw, and he organized a trip to the Metropolitan Museum to draw.

The curiosity and openness to multiple art forms, other cultures, and various forms of folk music spilled over into his teaching. I remember my drawings more than I remember any trendy or specific assignments or deep philosophy. He did one day in exuberance say "Everywhere there are rules and signs don't do this or don't do that. We need a sign that says YES."

So that atmosphere of YES healed my decade old trauma. Interestingly, my drawing became richer and more interesting when I was not trying to be more interesting or more provocative. I was focused on the marks and the darks and lights and shapes and movement.

Speaking of darks and lights, I agreed to plant sit for another student. She was living off campus with a few cats and a small jungle of plants. While I was picking up the key and getting the instructions, she showed me her studio space and her senior project. She had drawn a series of crows and ravens in lush and powerful blacks. Each work was at least 24" x 34" on off white or gray paper. Her work was elegant, rich, expressive and emotional. I have never seen anything like it before or since.

I was admiring her work. I must have remarked on her restraint in using just blacks, grays, and off whites.

"Oh, I haven't used color since my freshman year." She went on to tell me that one of her teachers had shamed her use of color in front of the whole class. From that moment on she had only worked in black and white.

There are a lot of assholes who are cruel. There are jealous and bitter people who find it easier to destroy than deal with their pain. There are people who should come with warning signs.

My friend seemed to have adjusted to the judgment passed on her. Aside from my belief that the teacher was at best misguided but more likely a person who inflicted violence on pretty girls with raw talent, did she benefit from not being distracted by color?

Or was her amazing work diminished by his unnecessary opinion?

I do not know. How can we ever know?

These experiences are why as a teacher I am always touched when a person shares with me what is concerning them about making art. Their fears may not be mine but I respect that it's getting in their way. And I enjoy holding the possibility for them that they will travel to the other side of that fear.

I may say the words that land just right, or I may demonstrate something that clicks or I may just cheerlead/encourage/mirror back how amazing they are.

Seeing someone create art from a place of curiosity and empowerment is incredibly fun. And gratifying. Creating your own art from a place of empowerment is life affirming.

Black Crows

# Collage Call to Action

Is there a color you like but don't use because it's too loud? Or too young? Or too old? Do you like polka dots but they are too silly? Do you like lace but it's too girly?

Or maybe you want to work only in black, but people say it's too dark? Or too depressing?

Do you want to make work about a secret? A story you can't tell. Or a story you don't remember but you know it's important?

Or you want to make a collage about what is holding you back/standing in your way/what has no solution/you don't even know what the problem is?

Find a bit of time to work in private.

Get a big piece of paper (tape smaller papers together) or open a large cardboard box – you want a large flat surface. Grab a fat black marker or a big black crayon – write all over your paper surface – write all the words – the words that hurt, the words you wish you had said, the words you wish you hadn't said, the things that can't be undone, the things that can no longer be done. Write out the secret as you need to tell it. Write out the story that you think it would be if you remembered. Tell yourself honestly if you knew what to do what would it be. If you knew what the problem was, what would it be?

If you are wanting to draw images, go for it.

Then rip up your paper, cut it up. Are there any words, shapes, thoughts you want to keep? Put them to one side. Shred or destroy the rest for your privacy's sake.

If you have energy, take what you kept and make another collage. Put the story pieces on the paper in the shape of a hill. Find a photo image of a person who represents you on the other side of the fear/trauma/shame/uncertainty/confusion/disappointment. Did you have a teacher or guide or friend who supported you in that journey? Do you want to add them?

Add images and colors until it feels complete. Sign and date your collage. Put it somewhere safe, where you can look at it but no one else can see it. Not until you are truly ready and even then I'd wait a bit longer.

Bone Mask

Cartography of Nostalgia.

# Chapter 8

## *First Prize in Second Grade*

Memories of the Past

The twins always wore the prettiest dresses. Their long brown hair was always braided with the prettiest silk bows. They stood together, sat together, drew together, and won all the art contests together.

I despised them. They were prettier and smarter and quieter and better liked than I was. Every time I saw them I felt my hateful heart pounding inside me. I hated their light, breezy, beautiful handmade dresses. Even though we lived outside of Chicago, I never saw them dressed in layers of itchy wool. I never saw them cold or covered in snow.

They drew exquisite tableaux illustrating scenes from the Bible. They lavished care on each creature, each fold of Mary's robes, each angel's beatific expression. They devoted their grade-school years to documenting important events in the life of Jesus, one award-winning drawing at a time.

While they documented the life of Jesus, I documented them. I captured their sweet smiles, their detailed white ruffled blouses and their pleated rose red skirts, not to mention their shiny black patent leather mary jane shoes.

For every soft delicate empathetic line they drew, I put 40 times the effort into my drawings. I liked a vibrant and saturated color. To achieve the rich hues that pleased me I had to press down on the crayon as hard as I could without ripping the paper. I'm pretty sure Jesus appreciates that kind of passion.

Every time their names were announced and they walked up to collect their blue ribbons, I heard the faintest laughter. It couldn't have been Jesus. Our teachers taught us the son of God was kind, not cruel. It must have been other gods, deities we hadn't yet met in our Religious Education class: gods whose complicated rules and histories wouldn't be shared with us until fourth or fifth grade. Capricious gods who enjoyed heaping beauty, love, fame, and good fortune on the awful twins.

Although I hated the girls completely, it never occurred to me to hate their parents. I didn't hate the mother who was behind their elaborate hair bows and handmade dresses. I didn't hate the father whose work had brought him from India to the United States. I am sure that second graders from Evanston to Mumbai found the parents inoffensive while barely tolerating their terrible daughters.

I am pretty sure even the teacher hated the twins and their endless first-prize ribbons.

To be fair, the twins were blessedly quiet – though it would have been hard to hear them over Kevin anyway.

Kevin had close-cropped hair that made his large, wide eyes look larger and wider. In spite of this jumbo visual field, his gaze was focused inward on personal visions. He saw a different world from the one the rest of us lived in. He always looked like he had just witnessed someone he knew burning in eternal hellfire. His expression comprised equal parts terror from what he had seen, vindication that his suspicions had been borne out, and commitment to saving your soul.

Kevin started the day by drawing and coloring crosses. Then he would carefully choose the best one to cut out of construction paper. He always had an endless supply of paper. A very intense day of soul-saving would require multiple crosses and perhaps some singing. But optimistically, he always started with one cross.

Once the cross was released from the confines of an ordinary sheet of construction paper, Kevin held it to his forehead and began chanting. His songs didn't seem to be in English. They sounded like what you would hear from a foreign congregation in a far-off country. He stomped up and down the narrow aisles between our small wooden desks. His heavy shoes created a serious, somber beat that was not always in rhythm with his chanting.

He never stopped in front of anyone's desk to ask or offer anything. But I could feel his ferocity in wrestling us back from Satan. He never spoke to us, so we never knew if or when he had the upper hand.

I never hated Kevin. I never despised him. No one did. No one seemed to give him much thought. If you got up from your seat, you had to avoid running into him – just as you would avoid walking into the teacher's desk or a door frame. That was about it.

He never did any of the work we did. He was left to himself.

Once someone asked why he didn't have to do the work the rest of the class did. I thought, "Can't you see he doesn't have the interest, let alone the time?" Maybe this kid wasn't in touch with his hateful heart like I was in touch with mine. But I figured we should let him continue his work, keeping us out of the devil's hands. After all, how many more drawings of flowers or turkeys or dinosaurs did the second grade need?

Second grade drew to a close and we were released for the summer.

As third grade began, a sense of confidence settled over our class. We had mastered our school's required skills in grade two. We knew how to walk in a single file, where to put our names on every page of homework, and how to raise our hands to speak in class. We knew that when the pencil sharpener was full, we were to stop sharpening. The student teacher emptied the shavings into the black metal waste-basket next to the teacher's desk. We all stopped what we were doing to watch. She put the sharpener back together and we continued our day.

We took in stride challenges that would have overwhelmed us in first grade. We relaxed in our wooden seats, confident that school was going to be the same. The same school, the same hallways, the same rules.

The twins were still in my class. Still winning first prize. Still wearing new beautiful hand-sewn dresses.

While the twins silently collected an endless array of first-prize ribbons, I was settling into my third-grade role. I had become a confident and athletic student – a School Olympian. There was great hope for my athletic future. The twins had the art world sewn up, but it was expected that I would earn Bronze or Silver medals at the next School Olympics. I stayed outwardly humble, but inside, I always had my eye on the Gold.

My athletic career ended cruelly with an extended and complicated bout of measles. The measles became strep throat. The strep throat left me with neck spasms. The spasms earned me a foam neck brace to wear when I returned to school. I wasn't able to do rolls or flips or even run very much. Weeks of sickness had compromised my muscle tone and my stamina. School Olympics passed by without me. I took up writing stories and focused on drawing.

Third-grade learning relied exclusively on purple mimeographed handouts. Perhaps it was the mesmerizing aroma of the mimeographs but we never objected to the endless repetition of sharpening our #2 pencils, writing our names, and circling, ticking, checking, and choosing. One worksheet had us circling all the words that started with TH, the next required us to check boxes and so on. The days passed slowly.

Three small hearts

By the time February rolled around, we were ready for any day that third grade presented, as long as it was like every other day. But Valentine's Day is not like every other day. And that year Valentine's Day was cruel in a third-grade sort of fashion.

Our teacher announced that we would be making valentines for our mothers. As the student teacher handed out red construction paper and crayons I felt my attention snap into focus. Ideas flooded my brain. I considered a number of options.

After the paper and crayons, we were given round-nosed scissors. Perfect. I would cut out a heart and glue it to a white doily, then glue that to another piece of red construction paper.

Inside I'd write a message. Mothers always read what you write inside.

My fingers tingled with anticipation. I was restless as a thoroughbred at the gate before the race, confident and ready.

The student teacher circled back. We were each given a mimeographed Cupid. The teacher told us to cut out the Cupid and glue it onto the red construction paper.

I was stunned. I looked at my fellow third-graders. Everyone was cutting out a Cupid. I felt sick. I missed Kevin, who had transferred to another school. Kevin would never have cut out a Cupid.

I cut out my heart. There were no doilies. None. The student teacher came to my desk.

"Do you need help cutting Cupid?" she asked.

I shook my head and she retreated. The teacher and the student teacher conferred.

"We are making Valentine's Day cards for our mothers. Everyone is cutting out Cupid and gluing him to the front of their card," called out the teacher. The student teacher standing next to her looked anxious.

The slow, pleasant, reassuring world of third grade was ripped away. I felt oppressed. Disrespected. Cupid was not optional. The senseless sameness and soulless copying were not optional. No one was leaving school that day without making the exact same card as everyone else.

The Cupid Conspiracy

I didn't have words to explain what was wrong. But I knew we weren't making art. I am sure even the twins knew it wasn't art. But they were obedient girls, and I think they went home and delivered their valentines with carefree minds and light hearts.

That afternoon, I carried the valentine home even though my hand burned with the betrayal of petty dictators. I had paper doilies at home. I could fix the card. But there was no way to right the terrible wrongs of third-grade tyranny.

## Collage Call to Action

I had to grow up to understand that conformity had its place. That the twins were not my enemy, that they weren't in competition with me. That humans feel safer in groups of sameness. And that my rebelliousness would allow me to hold on to my creative vision – even during the long years when that energy was pushed underground.

No matter what time of year it is as you read this, it's always a good day to make a valentine – and to make exactly the one you want to make, with all the colors and shapes and textures you want. To use the words and sentiments you choose. To celebrate the love you want to celebrate.

Our Velvet Hearts

If your card is for your significant other, your cat, your dog, or your goldfish - go for it! And please make one from you to you!

Use construction paper or gold leaf. Use doilies or diamonds. Use calligraphy or newsprint. Post it on social media or bury it in the garden. Embellish it with macaroni or leave it stark and to-the-point.

If you are not feeling lovey, send a Valentine's Day card to your snarky self.

If you feel too grown-up and sophisticated to make a Valentine's Day card, get out your crayons and markers. Use your non-dominant hand. Draw your love upside down. Let your inner child have some fun.

# Chapter 9

## *To Thine Own Self Be True*

Have you read any Shakespeare? When I was first exposed to his plays in high school, I was shocked to find that every sentence had cliches. Hadn't we all been taught that using cliches was lazy and unimaginative?

"This is supposed to be a great writer?" I said.

A helpful person gleefully explained to me that Shakespeare had invented the expressions that were so colorful and apt that they became cliches. His writing was much more impressive once I understood he created these expressions. I appreciate the person who saved me from my ignorance about his true talent.

It is astonishing how much he understood about people. He really was onto something with his exhortation to be your true self. It is a fundamental need: to know who we are and to know we are accepted and loved for being who we are.

But often we find it terrifying to be who we are. It can be painful. There are times it isn't safe. Sometimes it is illegal. Sometimes it is hurtful, confusing, and lonely. Sometimes offering your true self to others inspires them to kick you out of your home. Or to hurt you. Or to punish you.

I grew up with people who were not comfortable with the truth. They were also very private – especially about what was OK to share and what wasn't.

I learned to be evasive. I learned how to lie. To keep my equilibrium, I made decisions about who would know the genuine me. I vowed I would be as honest with myself as I could.

One way to do this was to journal. I was so secretive I used code words, especially for people. I didn't have a whole secret language or write backwards. My coding scheme was remarkably simple. And I didn't keep a decoder or lexicon. So when months passed and I reread my journal, I sometimes had no idea who I was writing about. Sometimes I couldn't even follow what I wrote because everything was so cryptic.

Rubies Nestled Within

A better way to express myself authentically was to create art. Even if I never showed it to anyone, I would at least be privately honest. In college, I did my assignments for the public, the teacher, and classmates. And for myself I did a series of collages. I explored my relationships to men - emotional, unreasonable, idealized, sexual. By today's standards they would seem tame but for me it felt safer to keep those collages private.

If you are depressed or anxious or feeling unsafe, it's important to keep your private art private. Honor your need for privacy. Listen to your need for boundaries.

One of the ironies of depression is that it robs you of the energy and clarity you need to extricate yourself from its damp leaden foggy grip. The further you have strayed from yourself, the worse your depression will feel. It's as if your logical self can't cope without your spirit's cooperation.

Rational logic is slow to respond. When it does, it often underreacts while your emotional side is overreacting.

You are lost, separated from yourself. Somehow your soul has descended into an underground world that has nothing to do with our material daily lives. The mundane details - returning library books, paying bills on time, keeping track of birthdays, details large and small – jumble up.

But the dark world is an important world with rich fertile fodder for artists, mystics and those brave enough to look at themselves.

Healing from depression always has mysterious elements. There are practical things to do when healing. And there are intangible, often impractical or illogical parts of healing. Doing art, trusting your inner self to bring you messages, and believing it is possible to return from this underworld have been pieces of my recovery.

Her Decision

Being too exhausted to dress, bathe, or choose what to eat is an everyday part of life with depression. Every time you can take even a small action you are declaring "This is who I am." Each of these declarations empowers you. And each declaration deserves your signature. Sign your work. On the front. It is an important part of owning yourself.

## Collage Call to Action

Gabor Mate is a Hungarian-Canadian physician and bestselling author who focuses on the effects of trauma on childhood development and the subsequent impact on mental health. He believes it is not just the event that traumatizes us. It is not having anyone we can safely tell. It is knowing that there is no one who will listen and believe us.

If you are depressed, there are stories you have not been able to tell safely.

Collage offers a way to tell those stories.

Collage is an act of selfness. When you choose one image over another, you are declaring "I make this choice."

Ask yourself do you choose black and white? Or do you choose color?

Creating art is a political act. You are not following the world outside. You are learning to listen to the world inside. Listening to the world inside you is a spiritual act of self-care.

As I have lived with and recovered from depression, I began by acknowledging I was broken. Flawed. Irretrievably damaged. Slowly, those mistaken ideas were washed off and replaced with slightly better ideas; I was broken and flawed but everyone is. Everything would be better if I could get everyone and everything into its proper place. Which eventually was replaced with: Who do I want to be? What do I want to give my attention and energy to? What is true for me (even and especially when I don't want to let others know)?

Silence.

Recovering from depression required me to make choices that moved me closer to who I am, choices that helped me learn how to speak to others. I learned to listen to the messages from my preverbal spirit. As I lived with this intention and created my art, I felt more comfortable being me.

I encourage you to use collage to tell your truths. *To thine own self be true.*

And I encourage you to play. To remain curious about who you are and what you want to say.

Keep what is private for your eyes only. Find a sketchbook. Write something tedious on the spine. "Cross Index of Expenses and Planned Debt Repayments." Open the book at random and write a rant of a manifesto in a bright crayon or marker. Use all the colors if you want. Write out your vow to be true and genuine. Use your favorite words, including curse words. Take your scissors and glue and markers and write "who I really am...." Then write it again. Write it until you've said everything you have to say.

Use your colors, shapes, and images to tell your stories in your sketchbook.

Remember: Reading about collaging is not the same as collaging.

Collecting materials is not the same as using them.

You will get the most value out of making things, especially if you do it consistently. Fifteen minutes every day will bring you more messages than eight hours once a month.

I have collaged in bed, on the couch, and at a table. I've cut out images lying down when I was too tired to do anything else. I've scribbled my darkest thoughts into a sketchbook, knowing I can cover them over when I'm ready. And I've authored stories I'm not ready to share with people using large letters that tangle and bump into each other and over each other so no one can read what I've written.

Grab your sketchbook, a crayon or marker and write in big illegible words "My life is not perfect, but I am freaking glad I am still here." Use your words. Use your biggest, sloppiest handwriting. Then glue down the pictures that rouse you out of the mire – I like the middle finger, women screaming at protests, me at the top of a mountain in Vermont.

Collage is always there for you. Three in the morning? No problem. Holiday weekend? No problem.

Collage welcomes all items – sticks from the park? A menu from that new restaurant that delivers? Old journal pages? Paper off an old crayon? Yes, yes, yes.

Collage encourages all makers. Are you a newbie? Join in ! Are you a seasoned collage expert? Join in!

A few final thoughts:

In these stories I have shared part of my world.

Having once denied the compelling call of my heart to be an artist and make art, I now embrace opportunities to encourage others.

Perhaps there is a compelling call that you are aware of that you deny? Maybe you want to discover what that call is for you? Maybe you want to influence others to live their best lives? Or do you yearn to make your world better?

Dream

Let my story inspire you to move toward your truest self, the self that has somehow gone missing. Remember all the ways imperfect people are moving toward who they truly are, even while they are in pain, confused, messy, unsure, or lost.

Go on, you are waiting for yourself.

Blackbird Singing.

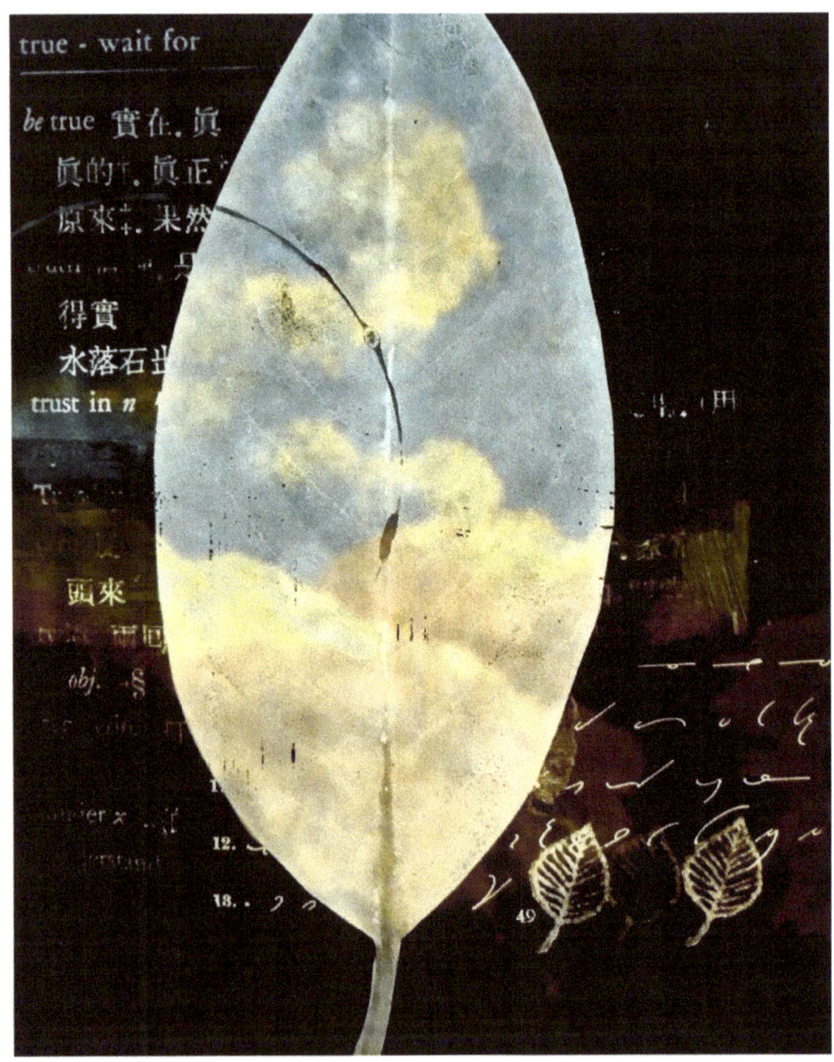



Trust.

# Alphabetical Acknowledgements

Amy Jarrett for the NO project.

Angela McEntee for editing.

Angelo for seeing me, especially when I was missing.

Brian McCormack for giving me my next project so I had to finish this one.

Chris Aiken, MD, for finding the right medication for me.

John Cohen, for bringing me back to mark making.

Julie Gieseke for suggesting we tear our papers with our teeth.

Julie Jacobson for having the largest collection of my art hanging in her home.

Mary Anne Radmacher for championing me as an artist in ways too numerous to count.

Mrs. Journet for starting my artist's ephemera collection.

Pam Lepley for asking to read my book and returning with thought-filled questions.

Patti Digh for telling me to slow down when I read before audiences.

Reverend Ed Brock for his foreword and his willingness to listen.

Reverend Peg Ashman for teaching me to gather the moments, no matter how hot the fires.

And all the wretches for inspiring me to seek higher ground.